big science
for little hands

squishy, squashy SPONGES

early childhood science guide for teachers

Art Credits

Photographs of live sponges obtained from Deep Sea Images.

Permission to use cover photo of *Being a Scientist* granted by Newbridge Educational Publishing.

Permission to use cover photo of *Sponges Are Skeletons* granted by HarperCollins Publishers.

Picture of live loofah plants courtesy of Peggy Moore.

Photograph by Paul Osmond of Deep Sea Images

squishy, squashy SPONGES

early childhood science guide for teachers

Editor

Mickey Sarquis, Director
Center for Chemistry Education and Terrific Science Programs
Miami University, Middletown, OH

Contributing Authors

Beverly Kutsunai, Kamehameha Elementary School, Honolulu, HI
Susan Gertz, Center for Chemistry Education, Miami University, Middletown, OH
Lynn Hogue, Center for Chemistry Education, Miami University, Middletown, OH

Terrific Science Press
Miami University Middletown
Middletown, Ohio

Terrific Science Press
Miami University Middletown
4200 East University Boulevard
Middletown, OH 45042
513/727-3269
cce@muohio.edu
www.terrificscience.org

Printed in the United States of America

10 9 8 7 6 5 4 3

This monograph is intended for use by teachers and properly supervised children. The safety reminders associated with experiments and activities in this publication have been compiled from sources believed to be reliable and to represent the best opinions on the subject as of the date of publication. No warranty, guarantee, or representation is made by the authors or by Terrific Science Press as to the correctness or sufficiency of any information herein. Neither the authors nor the publisher assume any responsibility or liability for the use of the information herein, nor can it be assumed that all necessary warnings and precautionary measures are contained in this publication. Other or additional information or measures may be required or desirable because of particular or exceptional conditions or circumstances.

ISBN: 978-1-883822-36-1

This material is based upon work supported by the **Ohio Board of Regents** (Grant Number 01-39). Any opinions, findings, and conclusions or recommendations expressed in this material are those of the authors and do not necessarily reflect the views of the funding agency.

Contents

Acknowledgments

The authors and editor wish to thank the following individuals who contributed to the development of *Squishy, Squashy Sponges.*

Terrific Science Press Design and Production Team
Document Production Managers: Susan Gertz and Amy Stander
Production Coordinator: Dot Lyon
Technical Writing and Editing: Dot Lyon, Tom Schaffner
Copy Editing: Amy Hudepohl, Jeri Moore
Production: Dot Lyon, Jeri Moore, Tom Schaffner
Cover Design and Layout: Susan Gertz
Illustrations: Carole Katz

Content Specialists, Reviewers, and Testers
Joan Ahrens, H.W. Wheatley Early Childhood Center, Capitol Heights, MD
Teresa Balsbaugh, home educator, Middletown, OH
Kathy Barker, Bear Elementary, Miamisburg, OH
Margaret Cassaro, Our Lady of Lourdes, Cincinnati, OH
Jerri Dollar, Heritage Presbyterian Preschool, Mason, OH
Gayla Epure, Durall Elementary, Cincinnati, OH
Gail Feix, Bauer Elementary, Dayton, OH
Melissa Hartman, director of Heritage Presbyterian Preschool, Mason, OH
Barb Hoffman, Middletown City Schools (retired), Middletown, OH
Betsy Kirk, Division of Education, Indiana University East, Richmond, IN
Karen Lawrence, The Seven Hills Schools, Cincinnati, OH
Sheri Maclam, Heritage Presbyterian Preschool, Mason, OH
Amie Minor-Earls, Middletown Community Education, Middletown, OH
Mary Neises, Bauer Elementary, Miamisburg, OH
Shirley Pomponi, Harbor Branch Oceanographic Institution, Ft. Pierce, FL
Jennifer Reffitt, Roosevelt Elementary, Middletown, OH
Nancy Stratton, Carlisle Intermediate, Carlisle, OH
Suzanne Stratton, Lincoln Heights Elementary, Cincinnati, OH
Matthew Sundermann, Bear Elementary, Miamisburg, OH
Connie Tschillard, Rainbow Schools, Kaneohe, HI
Janice Vanderplough, St. Joseph Orphanage, Cincinnati, OH
Ann Veith, Rosedale Elementary, Middletown, OH
Karen Vingris, Bauer Elementary, Miamisburg, OH
Colleen Wainwright, director of MUM's Tots Early Childhood Center,
Miami University, Middletown, OH
Mary Ware-Walsh, Evendale Elementary, Cincinnati, OH
Inge Watton, St. Bernard Elementary, Springfield, OH
Amy Williams, Bauer Elementary, Dayton, OH
Elizabeth Williams, Whitewater Valley Elementary, Harrison, OH

Foreword

Science is a way for children to explore, discover, and make sense of the world around them. When presented in a way that is meaningful for young minds, early science experiences provide the foundation for a lifetime of science learning both in and beyond school. Science learning is exploring, wondering, and discovering—it is not about memorizing facts.

The goal of the *Big Science for Little Hands* series is to help young children develop an understanding of basic concepts about the physical world and basic process skills that fit their level of learning development. How do children develop these concepts and skills? They need repeated personal experiences with materials and events from their everyday world. They explore materials, investigate ideas, and link what they discover with the world around them. *Squishy, Squashy Sponges: Early Childhood Science Guide for Teachers* builds skills for a lifetime of learning.

I wish you and the future scientists, leaders, and informed citizens in your care great fun while learning with *Squishy, Squashy Sponges*. Enjoy!

Mickey Sarquis, Director
Terrific Science Programs
Miami University (Ohio)

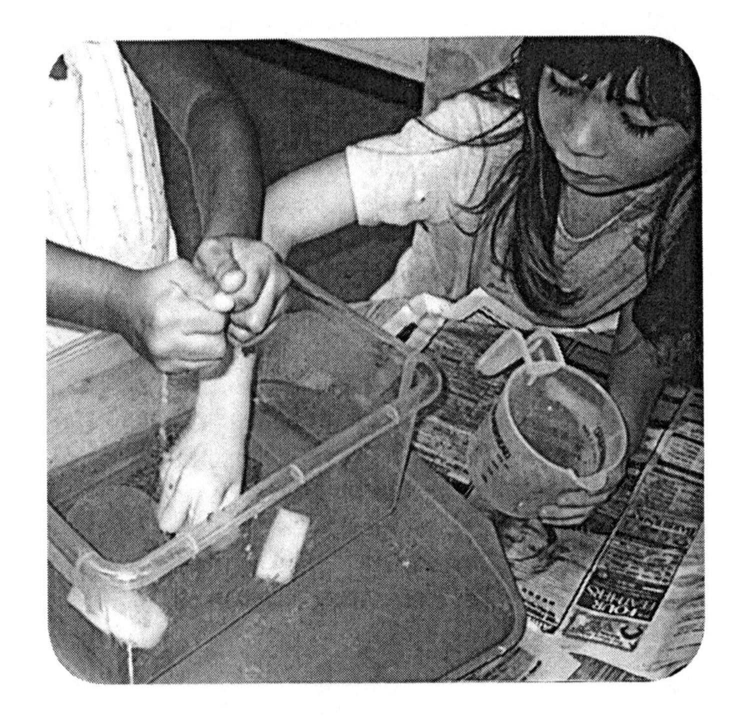

Using This Book

This section explains the organization of the book and discusses preschool learning, lesson planning, assessment, acquiring materials for the activities, safety, and setting up the classroom.

Organization of the Book

The book is organized in eight parts.

Parts 1–5 (learning cycle activities) contain 15 activities that address the four phases of the learning cycle: awareness, exploration, inquiry, and application. Advanced Inquiry activities are also included for children who are ready to experiment further. Each activity is presented in an easy-to-use format. (See pages 6–7 for details on activity format and pages 110–113 for a detailed discussion of learning cycles.)

Part 6: Sponges Across the Curriculum contains cross-curricular activities that relate the topic of sponges to drama, writing, art, biology, and cooking. To enrich the educational experience, teachers can use one or more of these activities at any time before, during, or after the learning cycle activities.

Part 7: Science for Young Learners contains information on developmentally-appropriate science instruction for young children, including why we teach preschool science, fundamental concepts and process skills, teaching with learning cycles, and documenting learning.

Part 8: All About Sponges presents interesting facts for teachers about natural sea sponges, including classification, physical characteristics, habitat, and diet. Teachers may want to share the photographs in this part with their students.

Range of Learners

Because preschool children are unique individuals who progress at their own pace, they reach the various stages of intellectual, physical, emotional, and social development at different times. Some children will understand all or most of the fundamental concepts about the physical world presented in this book (see page 103 for details), and other children will understand only a few concepts or none at all.

Many children will be able to answer the straightforward questions included in the activities, but the inquiry-style questions are likely to be more difficult for children to answer. In time and with practice, children will become comfortable with inquiry questions. Process and inquiry skills are challenging to preschoolers, but they can learn these skills and build the foundation for a lifetime of science learning. (See Part 7: Science for Young Learners for a discussion of inquiry learning and teaching.)

Lesson Planning

Squishy, Squashy Sponges offers a large selection of activities. The activities are organized by the stages of the learning cycle. Our goal is to provide you with a number of activities at each stage so you can choose what works best for you. For example, teachers wanting to designate one week to learning about sponges can select one activity from each phase (four activities) plus one of the Sponges Across the Curriculum activities. You do not need to complete activities on consecutive days, although you should present the activities in learning cycle order (awareness, exploration, inquiry, and application).

If your preschool uses centers, you may wish to incorporate Sponges Across the Curriculum activities and other sponge experiences as ongoing activities over the duration of the unit. This will provide children with topic enrichment and reinforcement. Center activities might include:

Science Center

- Make available a water table or dishpan of water near a hard surface (such as a table) that can be cleaned by children with various sponges. Children can explore and experience cleaning with sponges prior to participating in the inquiry activities.
- Do **Across the Curriculum 4: Sponges and Seeds** on page 94.

Art Center

- Make sponges and sponge paintbrushes available for children to participate in creative painting.
- Offer chalk and dark paper so children can draw and trace sponges.
- Do **Across the Curriculum 3: Sponge Painting** on page 92.

Math Center

- Offer rulers and tape measures so children can measure a variety of sponges.
- Have a balance and weights (such as small blocks or plastic counting bears) so children can weigh the sponges.

Block Center

- Provide various sizes of sponge blocks for building.

Housekeeping/Dress-Up Center

- Offer aprons, small amounts of water, sponges, buckets, sponge mops, plastic dolls, and baby tubs for children to role-play.
- Do **Across the Curriculum 1: Creative Dramatics** on page 86.

Writing Center

- Offer paper, crayons, washable markers, and pencils for children to draw and write.
- Do **Across the Curriculum 2: Writing to Learn** on page 90.

Assessment

Collecting children's ideas over time is an important feature of ongoing assessment. Examining student work helps teachers to identify patterns of learning for individuals as well as groups of children. This process also helps a teacher reflect upon his or her own instructional practice. Teachers can collect samples of student work as well as take photographs of and make notes about students as they work. Ideally, these examples, photographs, and notes are organized into a science journal for each student. (See Documenting Learning on pages 114–116 for a more in-depth discussion of collecting and evaluating evidence of student learning.)

As discussed in Teaching with Learning Cycles on page 113, the activities in the application phase of the learning cycle can be used for an assessment at the end of the unit. Teachers may also wish to establish evaluation criteria based upon learning objectives such as the following:

- Child can draw a sponge and show the holes.
- Child knows that sponges soak up water.
- Child knows that natural sponges are animal skeletons.
- Child knows that natural sponges live in ~~the~~ ocean.
- Child knows that people manufacture and sell man-made sponges.

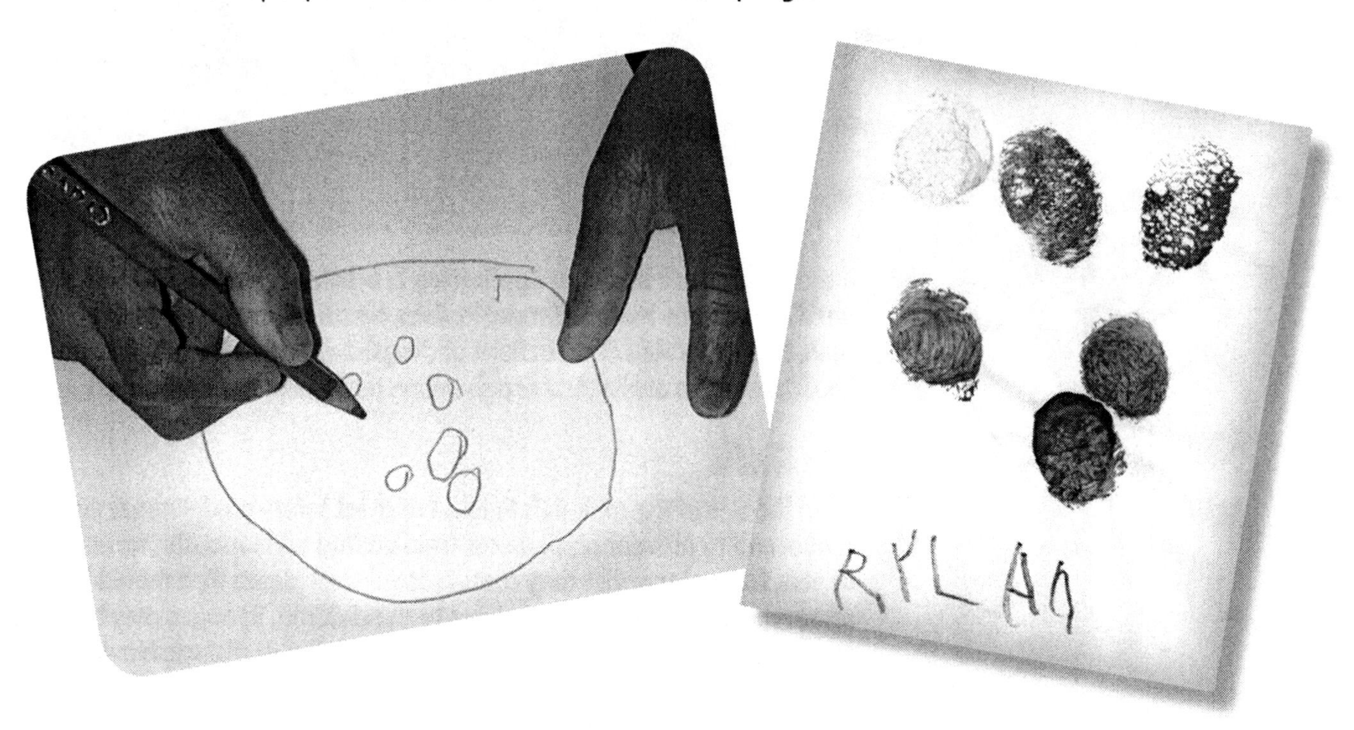

Above are two samples from a child's science journal. One is a photo of the child drawing his observations of sponge holes; the other is a sponge print. Teachers may use photos and drawings like these to discuss key features a student can identify about sponges.

A Collection of Sponges

A list of recommended sponges and online purchasing sources appropriate for all activities in this book is available at www.terrificscience.org. Try to have one sponge per child and several extras. Another option is to gather a variety of sponges locally. Visiting a local drugstore can be an easy first step. Other shopping stops might include the hardware store, supermarket, or discount store. Search for different types of sponges in the cleaning, painting, and cosmetic sections. Cooking stores sell pop-up sponges that are a great treat. Children and families may contribute more sponges to the collection.

If the children will be doing **Application 2: Is This a Sponge?**, you will need at least one loofah. Natural loofahs are usually available in the bath, beauty, or skin care sections of drugstores and department stores. Loofahs are also available through online retailers of bath products.

Be Safe

Keep the size of the materials in mind to meet safety guidelines at your school and to prevent small pieces from ending up in mouths, noses, or ears. Natural sponges may contain small shell pieces that should be removed before giving the sponges to the children. Sponges may be easily cleaned by adding them to a clothes washer or dishwasher with hot water and detergent.

Setting Up the Learning Environment

Learning in the early years takes place in a social context. The cooperation and collaboration that begin in these years are important qualities for learners of all ages. Plan for cooperative and collaborative opportunities in your unit. Encourage children to help each other while working together. They will discover more when they hear different perspectives and ideas and will practice listening to others' ideas.

Review the organization of your teaching space and materials to support active learning and collaboration. Select materials that encourage social interaction. Limiting the number of materials allows children to focus on specific items and prevents work areas from becoming too crowded. Limiting materials will also encourage children to set up systems for cooperation and sharing. You can rotate different materials in and out of the room as children need them during the unit. Include an area to display materials and examples of student work created during their exploration and inquiry.

Several sponge activities in this unit involve liquids, such as water and paint. Choose an area for children to work where they can freely explore the materials without being overly concerned about spills. Weather permitting, you might consider organizing some activities outside.

See each activity for the specific materials needed. If no water table is available, use dishpans or tubs. Other materials to collect ahead of time include assorted containers for water. Consider supplying plastic bins, aluminum pie pans, and other waterproof containers.

Remember that water weighs about 8 pounds per gallon, so be careful not to create overly heavy containers. Children do not need large quantities of water for these explorations. A small amount of water limits spills and can help children more easily keep track of what they are doing.

Paper towels are easy for hand wiping. Newspapers can absorb small spills. Bath or beach towels can absorb large spills and then be left to dry overnight and re-used. You can also use a sponge mop and pail.

Format of Activities

Each activity is presented in an easy-to-use format.

Learning Cycle Phase
Identifies the activity's learning cycle phase. (Details about each phase are discussed in Teaching with Learning Cycles on pages 110–113.)

Activity Title
Identifies the overall goal or theme of the activity.

Activity Introduction
Briefly describes the activity.

Duration
Provides an estimate of the classroom time and group size recommended for the activity.

Purpose
States the skills children will use and develop during the activity.

What You Need
Lists the materials needed to do the activity.

Helpful Hint Sidebar
Offers teachers useful tips to enhance or extend the activity.

Spotlight Vocabulary
Lists vocabulary words that teachers may want to introduce or reinforce during the activity.

Getting Ready
Provides teachers with instructions for preparing materials prior to the activity (when applicable).

Safety
States relevant safety issues to be aware of during the activity.

Awareness 1:

What Do Scientists Do?

Children identify the characteristics of being a scientist and are introduced to several of the processes and procedures that scientists use.

Duration

1 large group session

Purpose

- Communicate by sharing ideas about scientists
- Compare prior knowledge about scientists with information in a popular children's book

What You Need

- Children's book called *Being a Scientist*, available from Newbridge Educational Publishing; 800/867-0307; fax 800/456-2419; *http://www.newbridgeonline.com*

Although the student book version can be read to the class, the larger pictures in the big book version make viewing of the images much easier.

- Poster board or large piece of paper to record children's responses
- Optional: apparel scientists may wear, such as lab coats, goggles, wet suits, masks, fins, snorkels, zoo or museum uniforms, and hard hats
- Optional: equipment scientists may use, such as magnifying lenses, flashlights, tweezers, tool belts, and clipboards

Being a Scientist

Helpful Hint

Start a "word wall" for all new vocabulary words. Add new words to the wall before doing each new activity. Revisit the wall often.

Spotlight Vocabulary

- scientist
- experiment
- observing words (such as look, see, watch)
- measuring words (such as weigh, size, compare)
- recording words (such as write, draw, list)

10 Squishy, Squashy Sponges Awareness

Begin

1. Ask the children, "What do scientists do?" Record their answers for the class to see.

2. Read or show key parts of the children's book *Being a Scientist* to the class. Ask the children several leading questions about what the scientists are doing. Encourage them to vocalize their responses.

   Questions to guide children's thinking:
   > *What is the scientist doing in the picture?*
   > *How do scientists learn about things?*
   > *What do scientists use to learn about things?*
   > *How do scientists share what they learn?*

   Seen and heard:
   Children said, "They study dead things like dinosaurs," "They make things to help people," "Scientists help animals," and "They work in labs."

3. Return to the responses to the question "What do scientists do?" and ask the children if they would like to add answers to the list. After adding new answers, display the list in the room. Introduce the Spotlight Vocabulary terms.

Continue

4. Ask the children what scientists wear and use to do their job. Allow children to revisit pictures of scientists in *Being a Scientist*. Record children's responses on a new list. Display the list in the room.

   Questions to guide interest:
   > *Why do some scientists wear special clothes?*
   > *Why do some scientists use special equipment?*

   Seen and heard:
   Children said, "To stay clean" and "To see better."

5. Show the children actual examples of apparel and equipment that scientists might wear and use. Provide opportunities for dress-up role-playing by allowing the children to try on apparel or use the

Helpful Hint

Leave apparel and equipment in the dramatic play area for the duration of the unit.

Awareness

Squishy, Squashy Sponges 11

Begin
Lists procedures to begin the activity.

Guiding Questions
Includes suggested questions to ask children to facilitate the building of process and inquiry skills.

Seen and Heard
Lists examples of children's comments and reactions.

Continue
Lists additional procedures to continue the activity.

What to Look For
Offers children's reactions that indicate understanding of the topic.

Process Skill Power

"Comparing is a powerful process that can lead to the understanding of many important scientific ideas."

"Organizing is the process of putting objects or phenomena together on the basis of a logical rationale."

Lawrence Lowery, 1992

Process Skill Sidebar
Presents information about fundamental process skills that are emphasized in the activity.

Part 1: Awareness

What is the awareness phase?

The awareness phase provides children with experiences to help them develop a broad recognition of and interest in objects, people, events, or concepts.

During awareness, children

- experience,
- awaken curiosity, and
- develop an interest.

The teacher's role is to

- create a rich environment;
- provide opportunities by introducing new objects, people, events, or concepts;
- invite and encourage interest by posing a problem or question;
- respond to children's interest; and
- show interest and enthusiasm.

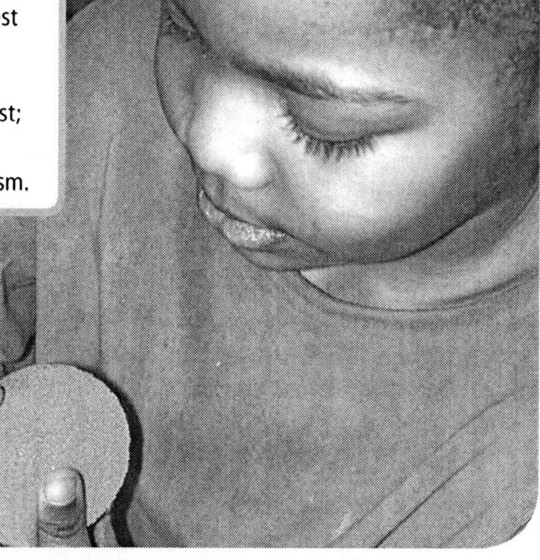

Awareness 1:

What Do Scientists Do?

Children identify the characteristics of being a scientist and are introduced to several of the processes and procedures that scientists use.

Duration

1 large group session

Purpose

- Communicate by sharing ideas about scientists
- Compare prior knowledge about scientists with information in a popular children's book

What You Need

- Children's book called *Being a Scientist*, available from Newbridge Educational Publishing; 800/867-0307; fax 800/456-2419; *http://www.newbridgeonline.com*

  Although the student book version can be read to the class, the larger pictures in the big book version make viewing of the images much easier.
- Poster board or large piece of paper to record children's responses
- Optional: apparel scientists may wear, such as lab coats, goggles, wet suits, masks, fins, snorkels, zoo or museum uniforms, and hard hats
- Optional: equipment scientists may use, such as magnifying lenses, flashlights, tweezers, tool belts, and clipboards

Spotlight Vocabulary

- scientist
- experiment
- observing words (such as look, see, watch)
- measuring words (such as weigh, size, compare)
- recording words (such as write, draw, list)

Helpful Hint

Start a "word wall" for all new vocabulary words. Add new words to the wall before doing each new activity. Revisit the wall often.

Begin

1. Ask the children, "What do scientists do?" Record their answers for the class to see.

2. Read or show key parts of the children's book *Being a Scientist* to the class. Ask the children several leading questions about what the scientists are doing. Encourage them to vocalize their responses.

   Questions to guide children's thinking:
   > *What is the scientist doing in the picture?*
   > *How do scientists learn about things?*
   > *What do scientists use to learn about things?*
   > *How do scientists share what they learn?*

   Seen and heard:
   Children said, "They study dead things like dinosaurs," "They make things to help people," "Scientists help animals," and "They work in labs."

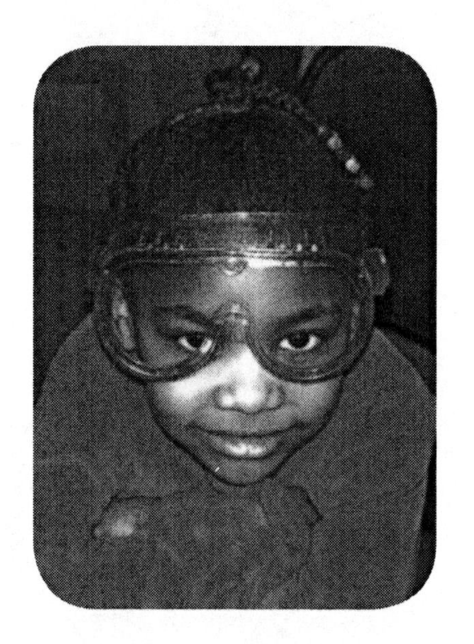

3. Return to the responses to the question "What do scientists do?" and ask the children if they would like to add answers to the list. After adding new answers, display the list in the room. Introduce the Spotlight Vocabulary terms.

Continue

4. Ask the children what scientists wear and use to do their job. Allow children to revisit pictures of scientists in *Being a Scientist*. Record children's responses on a new list. Display the list in the room.

   Questions to guide interest:
   > *Why do some scientists wear special clothes?*
   > *Why do some scientists use special equipment?*

   Seen and heard:
   Children said, "To stay clean" and "To see better."

5. Show the children actual examples of apparel and equipment that scientists might wear and use. Provide opportunities for dress-up role-playing by allowing the children to try on apparel or use the

Helpful Hint

Leave apparel and equipment in the dramatic play area for the duration of the unit.

equipment. As an alternative, children can put on imaginary props or draw pictures of scientists wearing or using the special equipment.

What to Look For

While some children will easily be able to vocalize their descriptions of what scientists do, others may have difficultly putting their ideas into words. Look for opportunities to provide them with the encouragement and time to participate. Showing the pictures in *Being a Scientist* should help the children describe their ideas.

While the children may not yet understand the meaning of process skill words such as "observe," "measure," or "record," they can learn to associate these terms with what scientists do. Look for children to use common synonyms for process skills (as indicated in the Spotlight Vocabulary) when talking about what scientists do.

Helpful Hint

Beginning each science activity with role-play can help engage children in the activity. Ask the children to get ready to do science experiments by having them put on imaginary clothing and equipment that scientists may wear and use.

Awareness 2:

Getting Excited About Sponges

Children begin their journey of discovery and learning by becoming aware of and excited about sponges.

Duration

1 large group session and 1 small group session, plus open play sessions

Purpose

- Become aware of and interested in sponges

What You Need

- Assortment of sponges varying in color, size, shape, texture, or other characteristics (Try to include both natural and man-made sponges.)

A list of recommended sponges and purchasing sources is available at www.terrificscience.org.

Be Safe

Sponges should be large enough that they do not fit in mouths.

Spotlight Vocabulary

- sponge
- texture words (such as soft, rough, bumpy)
- shape words (such as square, circle, triangle)
- color words (such as red, green, blue)

Let's Sing

Squish, Squash Sponge (verse 1)

(sung to the tune of Three Blind Mice*)*

Squish, squash sponge

Squish, squash sponge

See how they wash

See how they wash

They soak up the water for you and me

To wash and scrub our family

And tables and cars, as clean as can be

Squish, squash sponge

Squish, squash sponge

Big Sponge, Small Sponge (verse 1)

(sung to the tune of Frère Jacques*)*

Big sponge, small sponge

Big sponge, small sponge

We can wash

We can wash

See us clean the _______*

See us clean the _______*

Squish, squash sponge

Squish, squash sponge

* fill in with words such as table, sink, floor, and car

Begin

1. Explain to the class that they will be exploring some common objects they may have seen or used before. Emphasize that the objects are not to be put into mouths. Pass around the sponges so that each child gets a chance to touch, handle, and observe the various types of sponges.

   Questions to guide interest and enthusiasm:

   > *What do you notice about these objects? Use your senses but don't put the objects into your mouth.*

   > *Do you have any of these objects at home? How do people use them?*

   Seen and heard:

   Children said, "They get wet," "You wash them on your car," "I got a blue one," "I got a little one," "This is for washing," and "I saw a sponge in the sink."

Continue

2. Tell children that these objects will be placed around the room for them to look at and use.

   Some things you might say:

   > *Watch for these special objects in our room.*

   > *Be ready to share where you saw these objects in our room and how you used them.*

3. Place a variety of sponges in areas of the room where children regularly have time to freely explore and use the sponges. Suggested locations include the water table, housekeeping area, dress-up area, and art area.

   Seen and heard:

   While exploring sponges at the water table, children said, "Water is running out of the holes," "Water is dripping and coming out," "It floats," and "Bubbles!"

   One child used a sponge brush for painting at the easel. Other children wiped the table in the housekeeping area with sponges. A child said, "I'm washing the glass."

Helpful Hint

Children are apt to use and play with the sponges they find around the room in a variety of ways. Help children to do so in a safe and creative way.

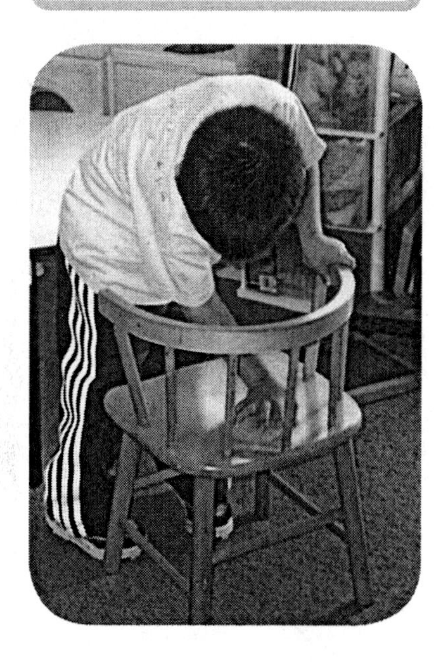

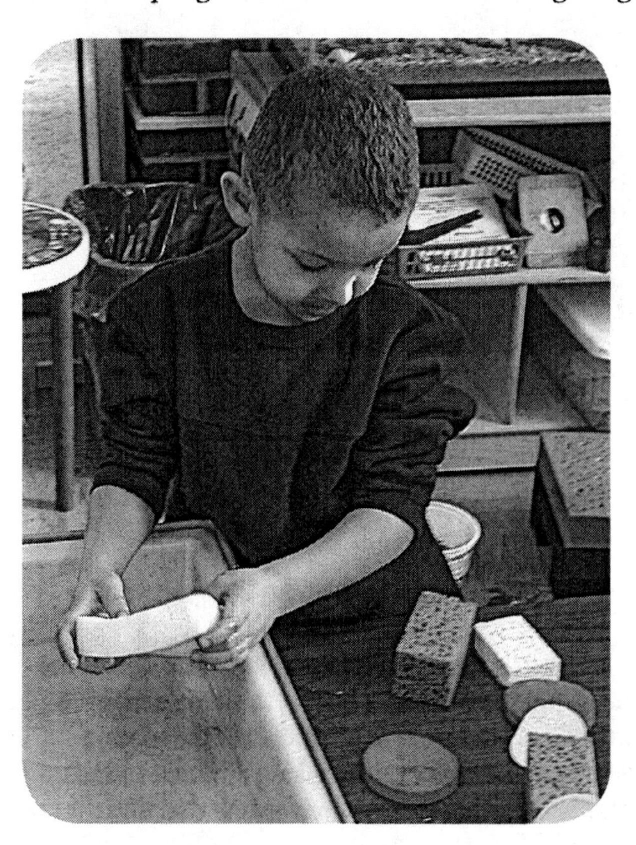

4. Meet with the children in small groups and tell them you are going to create a class book about the sponges they find around the room. Ask each child to go to one place in the room and get the sponge(s) they see.

5. Using one page for each child, write down the child's name, draw two eyes for "saw," draw a picture of the sponge(s) the child saw, and draw a picture of the location where the sponge(s) was found. Older children can make their own pages. Assemble the pages into a picture book. This class book will be used to introduce **Exploration 1: A Closer Look at Sponges.**

What to Look For

Watch for how children discover, use, and talk about the sponges. For example, one group collected sponges and took them to the block area. They enjoyed stacking the sponges and knocking them down. The teacher responded by giving the children a bucket to store sponges in the block area for further exploration. In another area of the room, a teacher observed children at the water table making different sounds (such as that of a motor boat) rather than using words to describe the sponges.

> **Helpful Hint**
>
> For the duration of the sponge unit, make a variety of sponges available throughout the room to be discovered and used by the children.

Stop and Reflect

Review with the children some of the things that scientists wear and do in their jobs. Review where children have seen and used sponges at home and in the classroom.

Guide the reflection process by asking

- What can you do to work like a scientist?
- How can you have fun with sponges?

Encourage children to describe the process skills they use to work like scientists using their own words. For example, a child may say that he or she "looks" or "touches" rather than "observes." Tell children that they will be working like scientists to learn lots more about sponges.

What to look for

Children should be aware of and excited about working like scientists to learn more about sponges.

Helpful hint

Some children are challenged by working in a large group situation and may be too shy to contribute. You can meet with small groups and individuals to help children understand that participating and contributing their ideas is an important expectation. They need to share their learning with the group and with you so all can learn more about sponges.

Part 2: Exploration

What is the exploration phase?

The exploration phase enables children to construct personal meaning through sensory experiences with objects, people, events, or concepts.

During exploration, children

- observe and explore materials,
- collect information, and
- construct their own understandings and meanings from their experiences.

The teacher's role is to

- facilitate, support, and enhance exploration;
- ask open-ended questions;
- respect children's thinking and rule systems;
- allow for constructive error; and
- model ways to organize information from experiences.

Exploration 1:

A Closer Look at Sponges

Exploring with their senses of touch, smell, hearing, and sight, children begin to get a "feeling" for sponges.

Duration

1 large group session

Purpose

- Explore and observe sponges using the senses
- Describe sponges

What You Need

- Class picture book from **Awareness 2: Getting Excited About Sponges**
- Assortment of sponges, including natural and man-made sponges, with distinctive colors, sizes, shapes, textures, and other characteristics

*A list of suggested sponges and purchasing sources is provided at www.*terrificscience.org.

- Poster board or large piece of paper to record children's responses
- *Sponges Are Skeletons,* by Barbara Juster Esbensen, or similar resource

Be Safe

Sponges should be large enough that they do not fit in mouths.

Spotlight Vocabulary

- sponge
- squeeze
- texture words (such as soft, rough, bumpy)
- shape words (such as square, circle, triangle)
- color words (such as red, green, blue)

Begin

1. Use the picture book the children created in **Awareness 2: Getting Excited About Sponges** to review what the children have already learned about sponges. Place it in the reading center so the children can review on their own.

2. Give each child a sponge. Discuss which of our senses can help us find out more about the sponges and allow children time to explore the sponges with their senses. (Remind children not to put the sponges in their mouths for safety reasons. This, of course, rules out using the sense of taste.)

Continue

3. After the children have had time to explore their sponges with the appropriate senses, have them describe their observations. Record the properties the children describe on a list. This list will be used again in **Exploration 3: Sponge Sorting.**

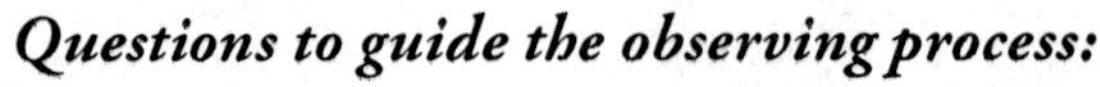

Questions to guide the observing process:

> *What does your sponge look like? Feel like? Smell like? Sound like?*

> *What happens when you squeeze your sponge? Drop it?*

Seen and heard:

Children with a variety of sponges said, "Soft," "Squishy," "Smells like soap," "This one feels like a marshmallow," "I see holes—little tiny ones," "Mine is scratchy," "It looks like a triangle," and "It smells yucky."

natural sponges

man-made sponges

4. Show the children some examples of natural and man-made sponges. Explain that the natural sponges were once animals living in the sea and that the man-made sponges are made in factories by people. Show the children pictures of live sponges from Part 8: All About Sponges. You may want to show and/or read pages 24–25 of *Sponges Are Skeletons* (which shows some differences between natural and man-made sponges) or a book with similar information.

5. Ask the children to look at the sponges you gave to them in step 2.

Questions to guide the observing process:

> *Who has a sponge from the sea? Who has a man-made sponge?*

> *How do you know? What makes you think so?*

What to Look For

Encourage the children to use texture, shape, and color words when describing their sponges. This should help them discover differences between the natural and man-made sponges.

Helpful Hints

Help children visualize where natural sponges live by putting natural sponges in the water table with toy fish, toy sea turtles, and shells.

Encourage children to compare the natural and man-made sponges while doing the other activities in this book.

Exploration 2:

Matching Up Sponges

Children take a closer look at their sponges as they try to find matching partners.

Duration

1 large group session, plus short daily sessions

Purpose

- Compare sponges
- Match pairs of sponges

What You Need

- Pairs of matching sponges, enough for each child to have one sponge

Each pair should have a distinctive color, size, shape, texture, or other characteristic to allow children to match them.

Be Safe

Sponges should be large enough that they do not fit in mouths.

Spotlight Vocabulary

- Comparing words (such as same/different, bigger/smaller, smoother/rougher)

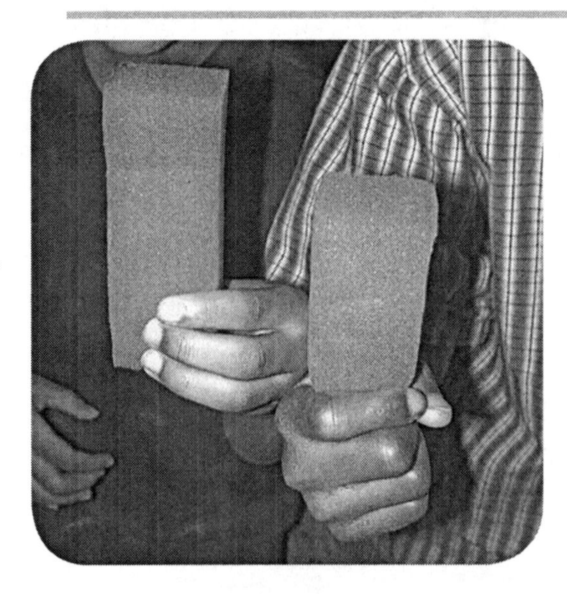

Process Skill Power

The comparing process of scientific thinking builds upon the observing process.

Matching is an early form of grouping, one of the organizing processes of scientific thinking.

Begin

1. Give each child a sponge. Do not mention the idea of pairs of matching sponges. Help children build on the observations they made in **Exploration 1: A Closer Look at Sponges** by identifying the similarities and differences between the sponges.

   Questions to guide the observing and comparing processes:

   > *What do you notice about your sponge? What can your sponge do?*

   > *Which sponges are larger/smaller, smoother/rougher, etc.?*

   > *Which has more/fewer holes?*

   Seen and heard:

   Children said, "I can squish it," "Use it for your body," "For your eyebrows" (see photo), "It can wipe houses," and "Do dishes."

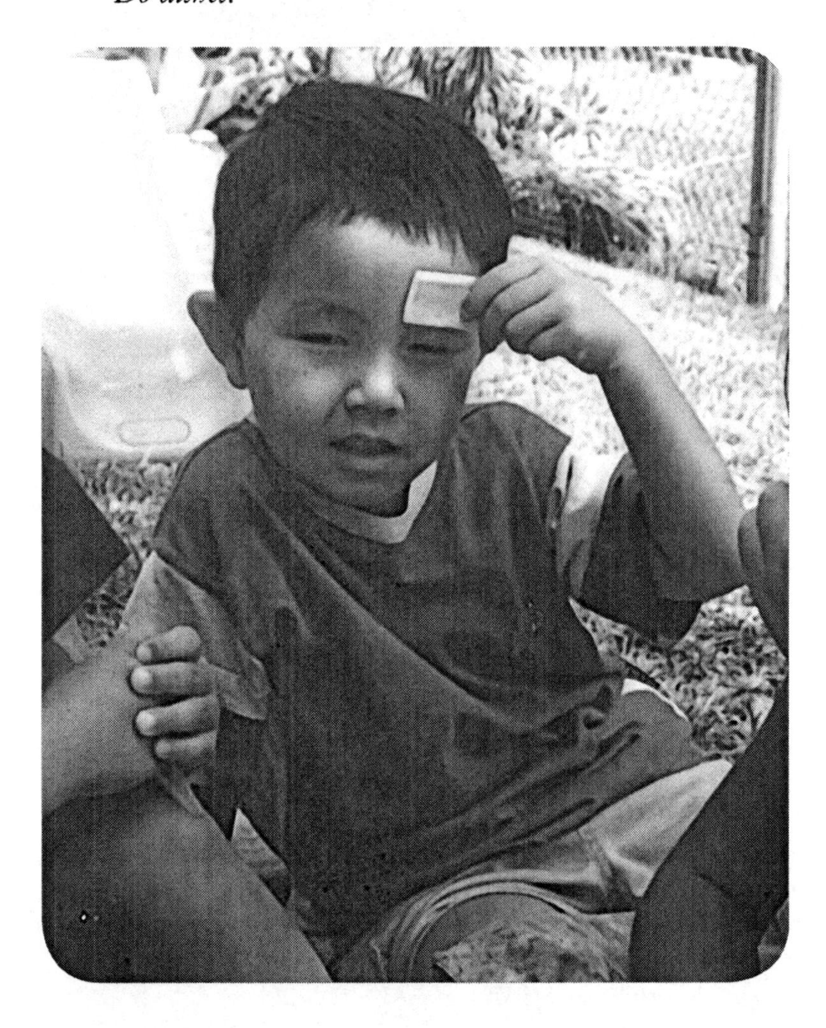

Continue

> **Helpful Hint**
>
> Children may need help to work together successfully. Take cues from partners who are working well together and share these with the other children.
>
> Cooperative skills should improve with practice, and children will get more practice in later activities.

2. Children will use the comparisons that they just made between sponges to help find matching sponges. Tell children that another child in the class has the same kind of sponge. Ask each child to try and find the other child who has a matching sponge.

   Questions to guide the organizing process:

   > *Whose sponge is the same color as your sponge?*

   > *Whose sponge is the same shape as your sponge?*

   > *Whose sponge is the same size as your sponge?*

3. Ask children to sit with their partners. Have the partners share their matching sponges with the class and explain why they match.

   Questions to guide the comparing process:

   > *How are your sponges alike?*

   > *How are they different?*

   Seen and heard:

   Explanations from three- and four-year-old children included, "They are purple," "We have rectangles," "They are ticklish," "I have little holes," "They have rectangles and pink, and you can wash with them," and "They are orange, and they are squares."

4. On subsequent days, continue practicing matching skills by examining the different attributes of sponges. Feature a "sponge of the day," and point out the featured attribute. Display a collection of samples and ask children to locate other sponges that have the same attribute. Children can also hunt in the room for other objects with the same attribute as the chosen sponge.

What to Look For

Children may match with a partner based on a single characteristic. For example, a child with a yellow, square sponge may decide she has a match with a child holding a yellow, round sponge. She could also have matched with a square sponge of a different color. No matter what characteristic you may have intended for children to use as a criteria for matching, be open to the possibility that children will use unexpected criteria, such as "prettiness." The objective is for children to have a reason for the match based on any characteristic they can observe and explain.

Exploration 3:

Sponge Sorting

Children take their exploration a step further by sorting sets of sponges into smaller groups.

Process Skill Power

"Comparing is a powerful process that can lead to the understanding of many important scientific ideas."

"Organizing is the process of putting objects or phenomena together on the basis of a logical rationale."

Lawrence Lowery, 1992

Duration

1 small group session

Purpose

- Compare sponges
- Group sponges
- Communicate observations of sponges through pictures and words

What You Need

- Assortment of sponges varying in color, size, shape, texture, or other characteristics (See Getting Ready.)
- List of characteristics started by the large group in **Exploration 1: A Closer Look at Sponges** (if available)

Be Safe

Sponges should be large enough that they do not fit in mouths.

Getting Ready

Select an appropriate number of sponges for the children to use in this sorting exercise. Younger children usually have more success working with a smaller selection of widely differing sponges. Children with more sorting experience can use a greater variety of sponges with more subtle differences.

Spotlight Vocabulary

- sorting
- groups
- observing
- comparing

Begin

1. Gather together a small group of children and read the list of characteristics started by the class (from **Exploration 1: A Closer Look at Sponges**). Place the collection of sponges where children can observe and rearrange them into groups based on various characteristics. Tell the children to put together all the sponges they think belong together.

   Questions to guide the comparing and organizing processes:

   > *How are these sponges the same and how are they different?*
   > *Which ones could go together in a group?*
   > *Why did you group those together?*

Helpful Hint

This activity builds on **Exploration 1: A Closer Look at Sponges** where a list is made of the children's descriptive words for sponge characteristics. If you have not done this activity, take time now to start a similar list.

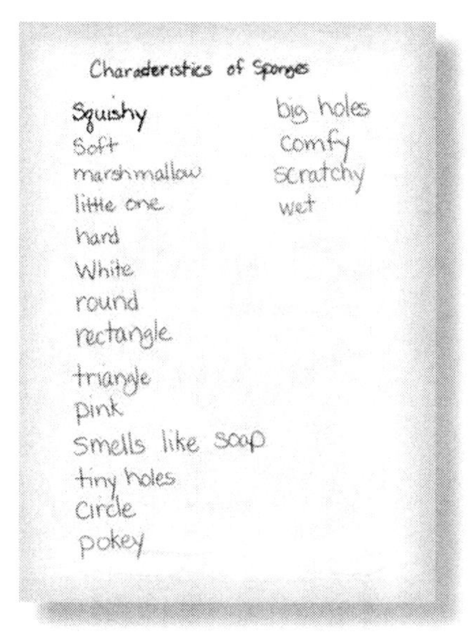

2. Facilitate the children's efforts to place sponges into groups by listening to and commenting on the children's observations. When presented with a pile of sponges to sort, younger children are likely to begin by pairing sponges that resemble each other and adding to those pairs to create groups. They often create a number of groups, each based on different criteria. For example, some groupings might be based on color while others might be based on shape. Older children may decide in advance to sort the entire pile by the same characteristic, such as color, until all the sponges have been grouped.

Seen and heard:

Children said, "They are round," "They have pink," and "These are rectangles."

Continue

3. Once children have sorted the sponges into groups, ask them to explain the logic behind their groupings. Leave the sponges in the groups for the children to refer back to during this process.

Questions to guide the communication process:

> *What can you say about how you sorted your sponges?*

> *How can you show what you found out on your paper?*

Seen and Heard:

Children said, "They look the same" and "They are pretty."

4. Have the children record their sorting ideas by drawing pictures, or write down their ideas for them. (Older children may also write.)

What to Look For

Younger children will generally create groups of items that are each based on a single property. Grouping items together (classifying) based on more than one characteristic is a more advanced skill that usually does not begin until age 7 or 8.

Be sure to let the children organize the sponges using their own classification systems; this will show you where they are in the development of sorting skills. You may want to offer more opportunities to sort as the children continue to explore sponges. The children will show you what they are learning and will become more comfortable as they practice. Take notes and check their continuing development of this concept during the unit.

Exploration 4:

Sponges Get Wet

Children will now informally explore another property of sponges: their ability to soak up water. This experience provides a foundation for more explorations in the inquiry phase of the learning cycle.

Duration

Short daily sessions

Purpose

- Observe the changes of sponges in water

What You Need

- Water table or tubs with a small amount of water for exploration
- Assortment of sponges
- Small containers that can hold and measure water

Be Safe

Ask children how to use the materials safely. Remind them not to put sponges in their mouths and to keep wet sponges over the water table or tubs. Give instructions for clean up. For example, children can squeeze out sponges and empty small containers before putting them on the shelf for storage.

Spotlight Vocabulary

- wet
- squeeze
- full
- dry
- damp
- empty

Begin

1. Ask children what they could find out by working with the sponges in water. Give time for free exploration. Monitor the area while the exploration begins to make sure the children are working safely.

   Seen and heard:

   While exploring with sponges in water, some children found that they could use sponges to pick up the water that had spilled onto the tray and then squeeze the sponge water back into the cup. The children found more sponges to use and "poured the water back in."

Continue

Helpful Hint

As children begin their work with sponges each day, help them focus on the topic by reviewing their previous observations.

2. After an initial exploration period, make the same materials available on subsequent days and facilitate the explorations.

Questions to guide the observing process:

> *How does the sponge change in the water?*

> *How does a sponge get full? What fills the sponge?*

> *How can you get the water out of the sponge?*

> *Does all of the water come out? How do you know when a sponge is empty?*

Seen and heard:

Children said, "It gets heavy," "I'm squeezing the water out, but not all of it is coming out," and "Squeeze more."

3. Once children have had ample time for free exploration, review their observations.

What to Look For

As you observe children exploring, take note of the various methods they are using to learn more about sponges. Do they ask questions of their friends about their work? What do they notice while exploring with the materials? Your observations will help you discuss with children what they've learned.

Exploration 5:

Sharing Home Samples

Children bring their experiences with sponges into a new context by extending the fun of learning to the home.

Duration

1 large group session

Purpose

- Look for and identify sponges at home
- Communicate about sponges

What You Need

- Letter to parents (A sample is provided in this activity.)
- Sponge samples from home

Be Safe

Remind children not to put sponges in their mouths.

Begin

1. Ask the children to locate a sponge at home, draw a picture of it, and bring the drawing (and ideally the sponge) to share with the class. Provide children with a letter to families explaining the project or have children help you write the letter. (See the sample letter provided at the end of this activity.)

> **Helpful Hint**
>
> Allow children who didn't bring their work from home to choose a sponge from the class collection to draw and share.

Continue

2. Gather the children into a large group to share their work. Before asking children to share, review what kinds of things people could share about their objects. It is often helpful for you to bring a sponge from home as well. Children can help you tell about your sponge; then they will be ready to tell about theirs.

Questions to guide the communication process:

- *What can you share about your sponge?*
- *What is interesting about your sponge?*
- *Where did it come from?*
- *How did you find it?*
- *Why did you choose it?*

3. Help children to listen to others' ideas, but also know that listening may be a challenge for them. Depending upon the age and attention span of the children, you may choose to break the sharing time into shorter sessions.

   Seen and heard:

   Children said, "It's shaped like a peanut," and "My Daddy bought it from the store." Some children traced their sponges on paper to share. Some drew the holes in their sponges.

4. Display the sponges and the pictures children brought to share.

What to Look For

As you listen to details about the sponges that children share with one another, encourage them to include key features and characteristics of sponges.

Dear Parents:

We are studying sponges in science. We've already looked at sponges in our classroom but would now like to learn more about the kinds of sponges used at home.

Please join your child in a search for sponges in your home. Once found, encourage your child to observe the sponges and tell you about them. You might want to assist in this observation by asking: Where did we find the sponge? What is it used for? What does it look like? What does it feel like?

Have your child draw a picture of one sponge you found together. Help them put their name on the paper and have them bring the picture to school to share.

Also if possible, please allow your child to bring this sponge to school to share. You can use a permanent marker to write your child's initials on the sponge, or put the sponge in a labeled plastic bag with your child's name on it. Sometimes sponges look alike!

We will be sharing our home sponges in class on this date:____________________ . Please help your child to remember to bring his or her work to school by this date: ________________________ . Thank you for your help.

Sincerely,

Stop and Reflect

Review with the children what they have discovered so far about sponges using the list of observations from previous activities for reference. Ask the children to share additional discoveries. You may wish to add ideas to the same list or start a new sheet summarizing their discoveries so far.

Guide the reflection process by asking

- What do you know about sponges now?
- What is interesting about sponges?

Tell the children that they will be finding out more about sponges as scientists would do, by doing more experimenting with them. Ask the class what they think they would like to know about sponges and how they could find answers. You may be able to incorporate their ideas into experiments during the next phase of the learning cycle, the inquiry phase.

What to look for

All children can contribute something to explain what they have discovered during the unit so far. Some may need to refer to materials or samples of their work for ideas, but all can participate while you record their ideas.

Part 3: Inquiry

What is the inquiry phase?

The inquiry phase of the learning cycle enables children to deepen and refine their understanding.

During inquiry, children

- examine,
- investigate,
- propose explanations,
- compare own thinking with that of others,
- generalize, and
- relate to prior learning.

The teacher's role is to

- help children refine understanding,
- ask more focused questions,
- provide information when requested, and
- help children make connections between prior experiences and their investigations.

Inquiry 1:

Soak it Up

Children watch a demonstration in which a sponge soaks up colored water. The children are then given the opportunity to experiment.

Process Skill Power

Reasonable guesses are more than simple guesses. Children can make a reasonable guess about the behavior of a sponge in water based on prior knowledge.

Duration

2 large group sessions and 1 small group session

Purpose

- Encourage reasonable guesses
- Observe changes in soaked sponge
- Compare soaked and dry sponges
- Participate in a controlled experiment

What You Need

- 2 small sponges that are the same size, color, and shape
- Clear, colorless cups with rims large enough for sponges to easily fit into
- Water
- Food color to contrast with the color of the sponge (for example, green food color with a yellow sponge)
- Permanent marker
- Assortment of sponges for the children
- Optional: zipper-type plastic bag

Be Safe

Sponges should be large enough that they do not fit in mouths.

Helpful Hint

Sponges absorb water at different rates. You may want to check the sponges you are planning to use and select ones that will absorb water quickly.

Spotlight Vocabulary

- dry
- wet
- squeeze
- full

Begin

1. In front of the class, add water to a cup to a depth of ½ inch. Add several drops of food color. (The food color makes the water in the cup and in the sponge easier for the children to see.) Mark the level of the water on the cup. Leave a second cup empty.

2. Show the children the two cups. Ask how they are different.

3. Show children the two similar sponges. Point out that the sponges are very similar. Tell the children you are going to put one of the sponges into the empty cup and the other into the cup of water. Ask them what they think will happen.

   Questions to guide the process of making a reasonable guess:

   > *What do you think will happen to the sponge when we put it in the empty cup?*
   > *What do you think will happen to the water when we put the sponge in this cup?*
   > *How do you think the sponge will change when it is put into the colored water?*
   > *What have you seen before that makes you think this might happen?*

Seen and heard:

When observing the sponge and water, children said, "It will explode" and "It will get really, really squishy." When observing the sponge and the empty cup, children said the sponge "will stay dry because there is no water inside."

4. Write down some of the children's ideas for later reference. You may want to have older children draw what they think will happen.

5. Place one sponge in the cup of colored water and the other in the empty cup. Let children observe what is happening to the sponge and what is happening to the water.

6. Ask the children to reflect on what has happened. Have them compare the two cups and sponges. Point out the line on the cup and the level of the water now. Read aloud to the class some of their initial ideas about what they thought might happen. Have the children compare these original guesses to what they actually saw.

Seen and heard:

Children said, "The sponge got fat," "It sucked up the water, but then it got full," and "The sponge turned green."

7. Hold up the wet sponge. Ask how the water can be taken out of it. Try several of the ideas the children suggest, including squeezing the water out into a cup. Ask the children to describe what happened.

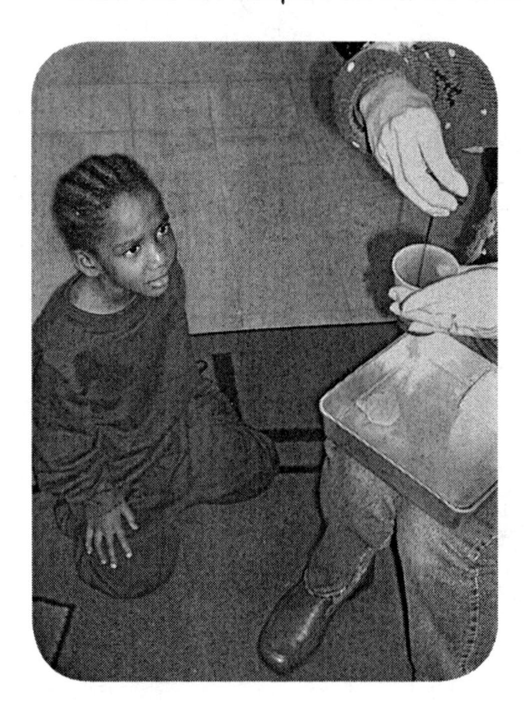

Continue

8. Working in small groups, give the children an opportunity to experiment to learn about sponges soaking up water and ways to get the water back out. Provide children with cups, sponges, and plain water (without food color).

   Statements to guide the process of inquiry:

   > *I wonder how much water your sponge can soak up.*
   > *I wonder how you could find out.*
   > *I wonder how much water you can squeeze out of your sponge.*

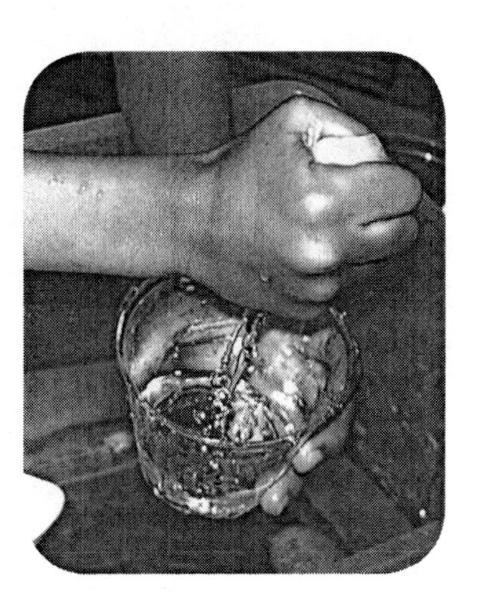

Helpful Hint

Older or more experienced children may be ready for inquiry involving measuring and comparing quantities. They can find out more about soaking up water with sponges in the advanced inquiry activities.

Seen and heard:

Children liked squeezing the water out of the sponges and into the cups. Two girls moved water from one cup to another with only a sponge.

9. Ask children to share with the class what these experiments have shown them about sponges. Add children's reflections to the earlier list of guesses.

10. As a final class experiment, set out several wet sponges for children to observe over the next several days. You can put one wet sponge in a sealed plastic bag so it won't dry out, and allow the children to use it as a comparison. Let them examine the wet sponges as they air dry.

Seen and heard:

Children said, "The sponge got hard" and "It's not wet anymore."

Helpful Hint

Remind children to check the progress of the drying sponge experiment each day. Help the children remember from day to day what they noticed about the sponges. Does this happen with all the sponges that are sitting out? Does it happen to the sponge in the plastic bag?

What to Look For

As you listen for children to explain their ideas about what happened to the sponge in the colored water, encourage them to use descriptive words and to provide details to explain their observations, predictions, and results. Look for children to explore these ideas further while working in small groups.

Inquiry 2:
Looking at Holes

Children take the observing and comparing processes a step further by recording and sharing their observations with pictures.

Duration

1 small group session and 1 large group session

Purpose

- Observe the sizes and patterns of holes in sponges
- Compare the sizes and patterns of holes in sponges
- Communicate observations of sponge holes by creating pictures

What You Need

- Assortment of natural and man-made sponges with various arrangements, shapes, and sizes of holes

A list of suggested sponges and purchasing sources is available at www.terrificscience.com.

- Magnifying lens
- Crayons
- Paper
- Scissors
- *Sponges Are Skeletons*, by Barbara Juster Esbensen, or similar resource

Be Safe

Remind children not to put sponges in their mouths.

Spotlight Vocabulary

- observe
- compare
- record

Let's Sing

Squish, Squash Sponge (verse 2)

(sung to the tune of Three Blind Mice*)*

Squish, squash sponge

Squish, squash sponge

See all the holes

See all the holes

Sponges are animals we all know

They live in the ocean to eat and grow

Their holes are tunnels where water flows

Squish, squash sponge

Squish, squash sponge

Big Sponge, Small Sponge (verse 2)

(sung to the tune of Frère Jacques*)*

Big sponge, small sponge

Big sponge, small sponge

See the holes

See the holes

Sponges are animals*

Sponges are animals*

Squish, squash sponge

Squish, squash sponge

* repeat song two times, replacing with "Sponges are skeletons" and then "Sponges have tunnels."

Begin

1. In small groups, have children observe the different types of holes in sponges. Ask the children to compare the holes in the sea sponges with the holes in the man-made sponges. Have them take a closer look with a magnifying lens.

   Question to guide the observing and comparing process:

   > *What do you notice about the holes?*

   Seen and heard:

   Children said, "I see big and little holes" and "I have tiny holes."

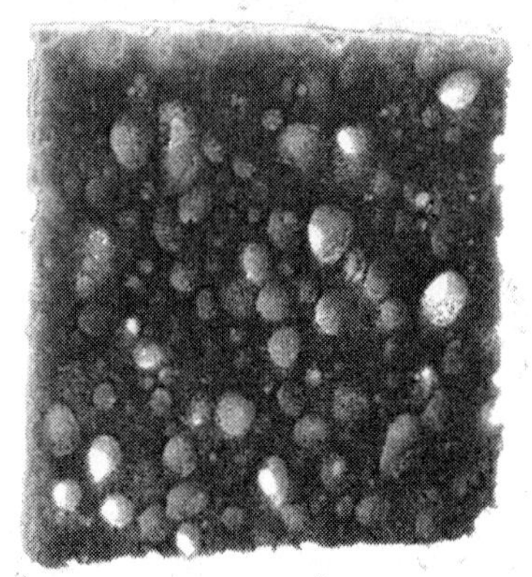

sponge slice

2. To help children look at the holes another way, use scissors to cut a slice of sponge about ¼-inch thick. Hold the slice up to a sunny window and let children see how the light shines through the holes.

3. Read and show pictures to the children from pages 12–15 of *Sponges Are Skeletons* (or a book with similar information), which shows how live sponges use their holes.

Continue

4. Tell children that one way for scientists to share their observations is with pictures. Ask the children to record their observations by drawing a picture of a sponge showing the holes, drawing a picture of one hole, or making a sponge cutout by folding a piece of paper and cutting out holes.

5. Have children share their drawings and cutouts with the class.

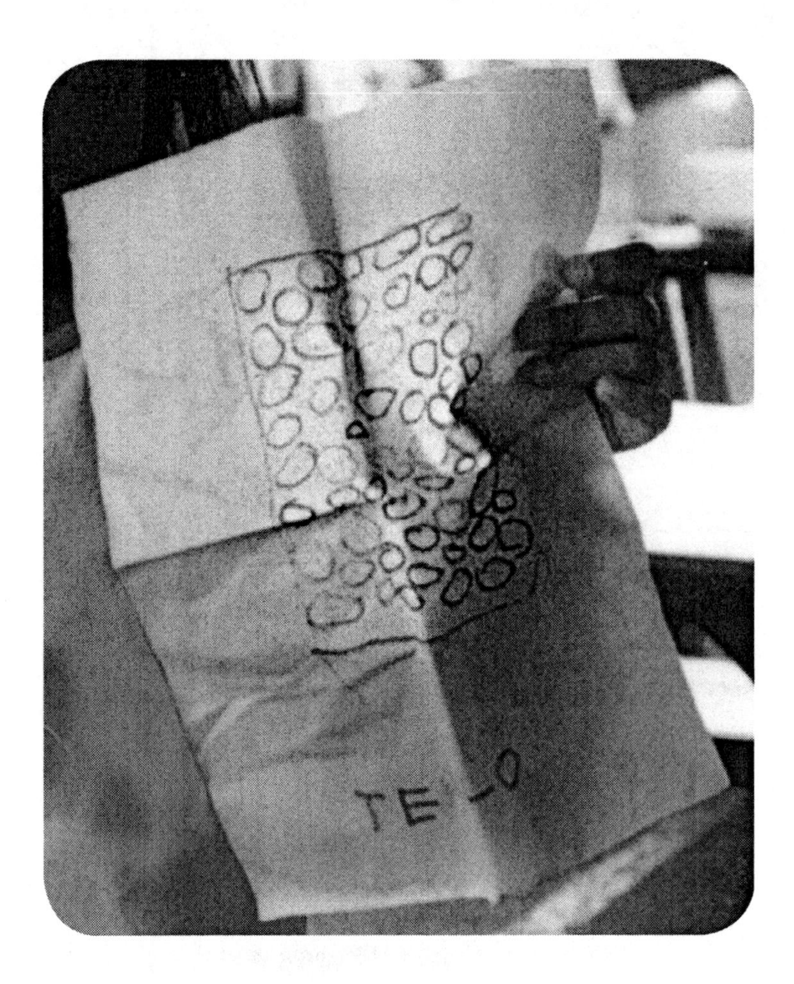

Questions to guide the discussion:

> *Why did you draw the holes the way that you did?*

> *How is your picture different from your sponge?*

> *How is your picture the same as your sponge?*

> *Compare your picture to another person's picture. What do you notice?*

Seen and heard:

Children said, "The holes are circles" and "Mine is bigger."

What to Look For

Listen for children to notice that sponge holes are different sizes. Look for children to draw or cut out shapes to represent their sponges. During the sharing session, encourage the children to make comparisons of holes in their sponges with holes in other sponges.

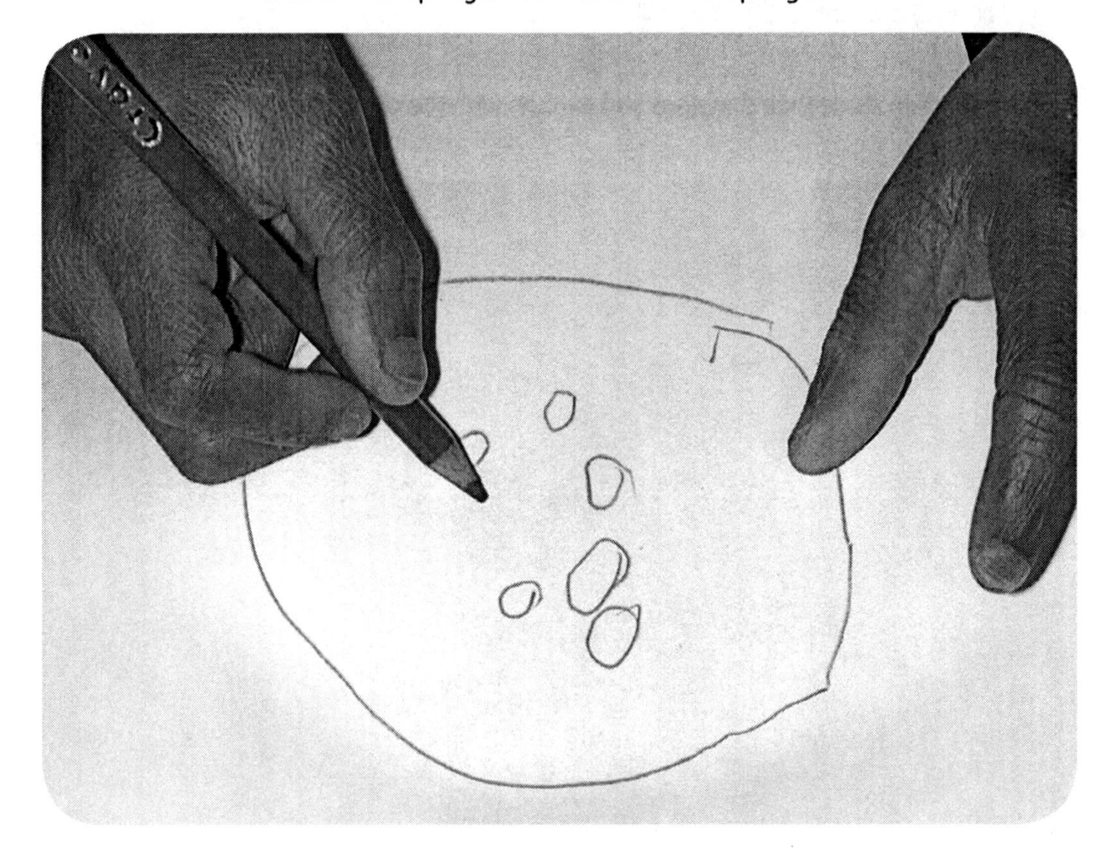

Inquiry 3:

Printing Holes

Children get a different perspective on the holes in sponges by making and sorting sponge prints.

Duration

2 small group sessions

Purpose

- Observe the sizes and patterns of holes in sponges
- Compare the sizes and patterns of holes in sponges
- Match sponges to their corresponding prints
- Sort sponge prints

What You Need

- Assortment of natural and man-made sponges with various arrangements, shapes, and sizes of holes
- Tempera paint or other washable paint
- Flat containers to hold paint, such as foam meat trays or aluminum pie pans
- Paper
- Optional: clothespins

Be Safe

Sponges should be large enough that they do not fit in mouths.

Getting Ready

Clothespins can be clipped to the sponges for children to use as handles. (See photo.) Be aware that the paint may stain the sponges or leave a paint residue that is slow to disappear.

Spotlight Vocabulary

- size words (such as big, large, small, tiny, little, medium)
- shape words (such as round, square, like a circle)

Process Skill Power

Sorting picture representations of objects involves higher thinking skills than sorting the actual objects.

Begin

1. With a small group of children, demonstrate the process of dipping the sponge into the paint and pressing it to the paper to print. Remind the children that because they want to make a print that shows the holes of the sponge, they should not move the sponge from side to side while printing on the paper.

2. Provide small sheets of paper. Ask children to put their names on their papers. (For younger children, write names in advance.) Have children make prints of various sponges.

   Questions to guide the observing, comparing, and communicating processes:

   > *How do the printed holes compare to the real holes?*

   > *Describe how you made your best prints.*

   Seen and heard:

   Children said, "I put it down and it sticks" and "It's pretty."

3. Clean the sponges and allow the sponges and prints to dry.

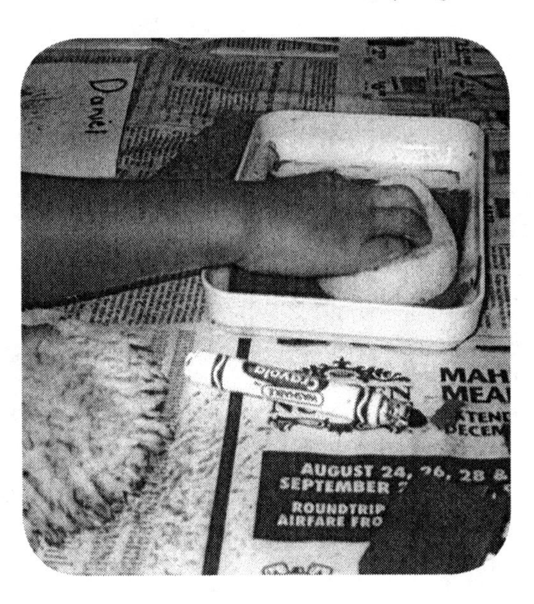

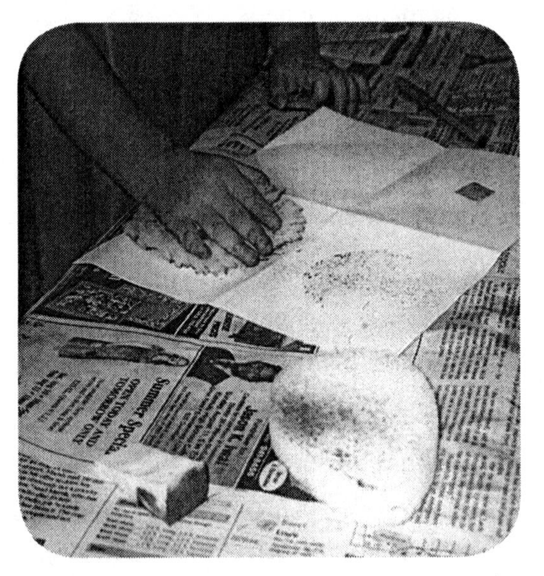

Continue

4. Have the children work in small groups to match sponges with corresponding prints.

   Question to guide the observing, comparing, and matching process:

   > *What clues helped you match the sponges to their prints?*

   Seen and heard:

   Children said, "It's a circle" and "I see big holes."

5. Have the children repeat the sorting activity described in **Exploration 3: Sponge Sorting,** but this time use only the sponge prints. Now the children will be using picture representations of the sponges they previously manipulated. This task involves the higher thinking skills of transferring generalizations about actual three-dimensional objects to two-dimensional representations of the objects.

   Question to guide the observing, comparing, and matching processes:

   > *What about the sponge prints helped you sort them?*

   Seen and heard:

   Children said, "That's a big one" and "Rectangles."

What to Look For

Look for children to match the sponge prints to the sponges primarily based on shape and size. Some children will notice the variation in hole shapes, sizes, and quantity. Help the children to vocalize the factors they used in both the matching and sorting of sponge prints.

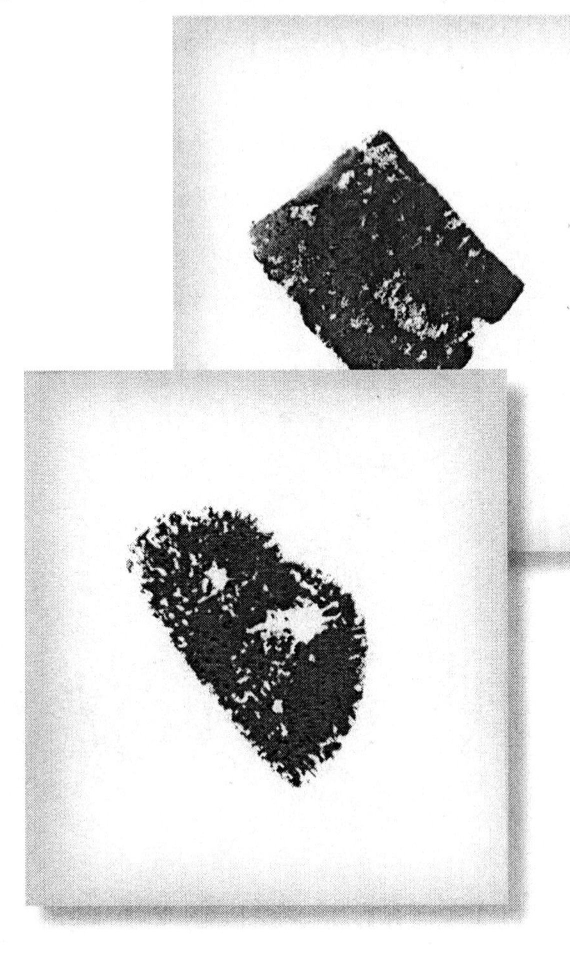

Inquiry 4:

I Wonder...

Children participate in self-discovery activities with or about sponges.

Duration

2 large group sessions and 1 small group session

Purpose

- Learn the process of self-discovery by asking questions, planning and doing investigations, and recording results
- Communicate results to the class

What you Need

- Assortment of natural and man-made sponges

A list of suggested sponges and sources for purchasing is available at www.terrificscience.com.

- I Wonder Data Sheet for each child (A sample is provided in this activity.)
- Materials determined by the children

Be Safe

Remind children not to put sponges in their mouths.

Spotlight Vocabulary

- float
- sink
- plan
- test
- wonder
- record

Process Skill Power

"What separates true inquiry from play are the processes of observing and questioning, and then developing and following a plan of action."

Jane Bresnick, 2000

Activity adapted from inquiry learning information in *Connect*, March/April 2000, *13*(4), 1–8. *http://www.synergylearning.org*

Begin

1. Gather the children together and ask them to share what they have learned about sponges so far. Explain that while they have already learned a lot about sponges, there is still a lot more to discover. Model the inquiry process by making an "I wonder" statement that is easily testable. For example, "I wonder if sponges sink or float in water." Write down your "I wonder" statement on an I Wonder Data Sheet for the children to see. (See the sample data sheet provided at the end of this activity.) Ask the children to come up with a plan for testing your statement. Draw a picture depicting the plan on the "What I Plan to Do" section of the data sheet.

   Questions to guide the inquiry:

   > *How can we test what I am wondering about?*

   > *What things do we need for our test?*

Helpful Hint

If you choose to test the suggested question about sinking and floating sponges, encourage the children to include both natural and man-made sponges in the testing plan.

Results will vary depending on the children's test. Generally, all dry sponges float at first. When sponges are submerged in water, squeezed to remove air bubbles, and released, the man-made sponges tend to float and the natural sponges tend to sink.

2. As a class, conduct the test outlined by the children. With the help of the children, complete the "What I Found Out" section of the data sheet.

Continue

3. Ask the children what other things they wonder about sponges. It may be helpful to review with the children the previous sponge activities that they did. Ask the children to describe the procedures and the results.

4. Working in small groups, ask the children to come up with their own "I wonder" statement that relates to sponges. Ask the children to come up with a plan for testing their statement, and draw it on the "What I Plan to Do" portion of the data sheet.

   Questions to guide the inquiry process:

   > *What do you wonder about sponges?*

   > *How can you test your idea?*

   > *What do you need to use for your test?*

Helpful Hints

Allow the children to come up with their own plan for testing the "I wonder" statement. The investigation process is more meaningful to children when they design and implement their own procedures rather than use procedures outlined by the teacher.

During the inquiry process, the teacher should observe, question, and support the efforts of the children. Some redirecting of the children's plan may be necessary. You may also have to assist some children who have a hard time articulating their ideas by helping them find the right words.

5. Have the children conduct their test, and then assist each child as needed in drawing and writing to complete the "What I Found Out" portion of the data sheet.

6. Gather the children together and ask each group of children to show their data sheets and describe their findings to the class.

What to Look For

Mastering the inquiry learning process takes lots of time and practice. Some children may have difficulty with all or some of the questioning, planning, testing, and recording steps. Modeling the process and working with children in small groups will help them learn the inquiry process.

I Wonder Data Sheet

big science
for little hands

Name ______________________________

I wonder ______________________________

____

What I Plan to Do

What I Found Out

Stop and Reflect

Set up an exhibit of the children's sponge prints. In small groups, meet with the children to view and discuss the exhibit. Record their ideas and add them to the display for others to see. Read their ideas aloud and share them with the class.

Guide the discussion process by asking

- What do you think about your own work?
- What do you notice about sponges by looking at the group's work?
- What do you want to remember about sponges?
- What was something new that you learned by doing these activities?
- What is important to remember about holes in sponges?

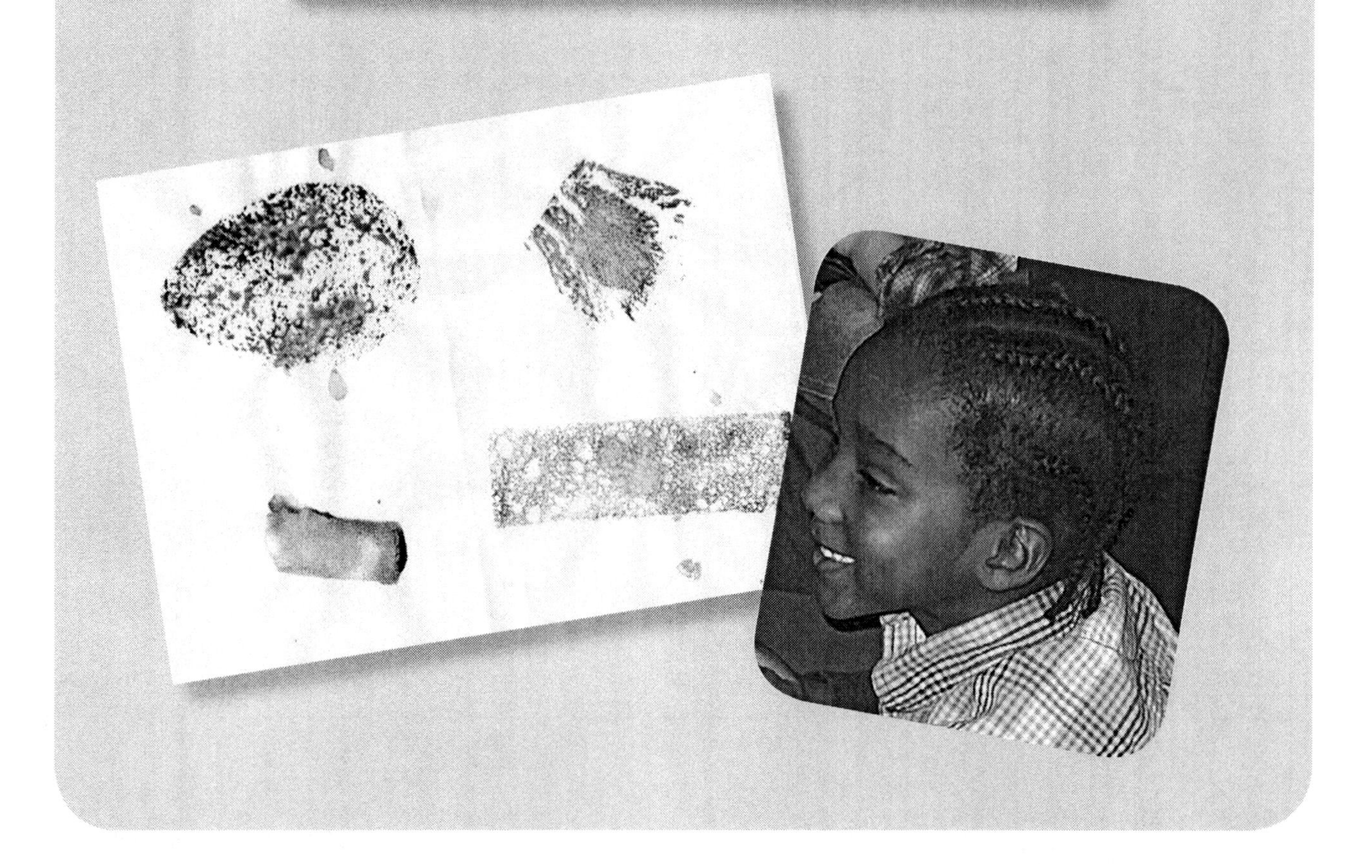

Part 4: Advanced Inquiry

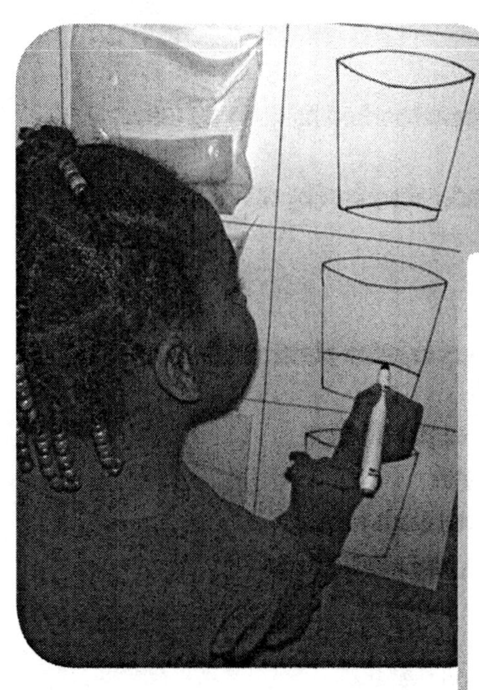

How are advanced inquiry activities different?

The advanced inquiry activities expand early measuring skills (which focus on comparing objects to one another) to include comparing objects to both nonstandard and standard units of measure.

Each activity in this section begins with teachers modeling inquiry that involves measurement. Later steps allow children to continue the inquiry process on their own.

Advanced Inquiry 1:

How Much Water?

Children investigate and compare the amounts of water that various sponges absorb.

> **Helpful Hint**
>
> This activity builds on **Exploration 4: Sponges Get Wet.** You may want to refresh the children's memory through free play to give them a chance to see how sponges behave in water.

Duration

1 small group session and 1 large group session, plus individual investigations

Purpose

- Measure the amount of water absorbed by sponges using arbitrary units of measure
- Compare the amount of water absorbed by different sponges

What You Need

- Assortment of sponges
- 1-quart plastic deli containers or other plastic wide-mouth containers
- Clear or translucent 10-ounce plastic cups
- Water table or a tub and water
- Paper towels, newspaper, and cloth towels
- Poster board, markers, tape, and plastic bags

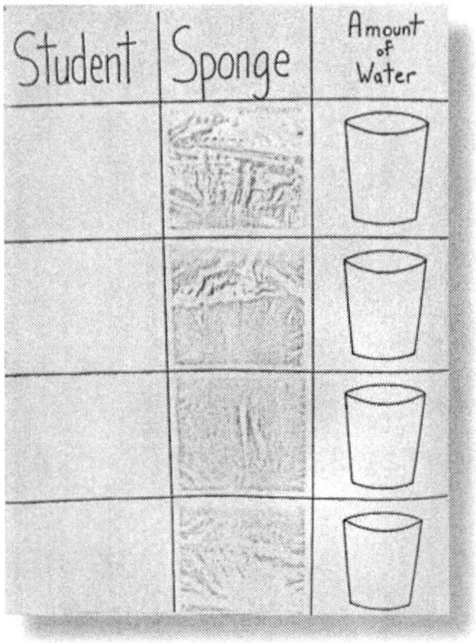

Be Safe

Sponges should be large enough that they do not fit in mouths.

Getting Ready

Create a chart to record children's results. (See photo.) Tape plastic bags to the chart to later display the children's sponges. Draw empty cups on the chart so that the children can draw lines to represent water levels.

Student	Sponge	Amount of Water

Spotlight Vocabulary

- wet
- absorb
- measure
- full
- empty

Begin

1. Working in small groups, explain to the children that they will be comparing the amounts of water that different sponges can soak up. Explain that, as part of being good scientists, everyone needs to agree on one rule for deciding if a sponge has soaked up all the water it can (if it is full) and another rule for deciding if nearly all the water has been squeezed out of a sponge (if it is empty).

2. Give children an opportunity to play with sponges in the water table or tub of water and come up with ways to decide if a sponge is full or empty. Have them practice filling and emptying sponges.

   Questions to guide the discussion:

   > *How do you know when a sponge is full?*

   > *How do you know when a sponge is empty?*

   Seen and heard:

   Children said, "'Cause it drips," "Because it bends on my fingers," "You can see the drops," "The sponge was full and fat," "It gets bigger," and "It's wet and squishy." Then children said, "It's starting to get dry" and "It stops dripping."

Continue

3. Have each child fill a sponge with water using the water table or tub of water and then empty the sponge into an empty deli container or other container with a wide mouth.

4. Have children pour the water from the deli container into the 10-ounce cup and then mark the height of the water. (Squeezing water from the sponges into wide-mouth containers is easier for the children, but the wide shape makes differences in water amounts hard to see. Pouring water into a narrower cup makes comparing amounts easier.)

5. Help the children relate the amount of water in the cup to the idea of how much each sponge can hold.

6. Have children write their names on the chart, hang their sponges in the plastic bags, and draw lines on the chart's cups to represent the height of water in their cups. (You may want to fill out the chart for younger children.) Discuss the results.

Helpful Hint

If these displays are going to last several days, be sure to leave the tops of the bags open so that the sponges don't get musty.

7. Once all the children have had a chance to complete the activity and add their information to the chart, meet as a class to review and discuss the results.

   Questions to guide the observing and comparing processes:

   > *Did all the sponges hold the same amount of water? How do you know?*

   > *Which sponge held the most water? The least water?*

   > *What do you notice about sponges that hold more water than others? Are they bigger? Smaller? Softer? Stiffer? Sea sponges? Man-made sponges? What do you notice about sponges that hold less water than others?*

8. Give children the opportunity to continue this investigation on their own.

   Questions to guide the investigation:

   > *What do you wonder about sponges and how much water they hold?*

   > *How could you find out?*

   > *What did you do to find out?*

   > *What happened?*

   > *Do you wonder about anything else now?*

   Seen and heard:

   Children said, "Squeezed out the water," "Drew on the cups," and "Can you put milk in them?"

What to Look For

During the inquiry steps and class discussion, look for indications that children understand the relationship between the amount of water squeezed into a container and how much water a sponge can hold. If children have problems with this concept, repeat the activity and help them squeeze the water directly from the sponge into the 10-ounce cup. This will remove the distraction of an intermediate collection vehicle.

When children continue the investigation on their own, watch for those who can set up a system to experiment with the objects and keep track of their results. Listen for comments and questions that children ask each other as they are working. Observe how children work cooperatively and collaboratively during this activity.

Advanced Inquiry 2:

How Heavy Is the Water?

Children investigate and compare the weights of various sponges when dry and wet.

Duration

1 small group session and 1 large group session, plus individual investigations

Purpose

- Match the weights of dry and wet sponges to objects
- Watch the balance to see when the weights of two objects match
- Compare the weights of sponges when dry and wet
- Count the number of objects that match a sponge's weight

What You Need

- 2 primary or bucket balances
- Assortment of dry sponges
- Set of weights (such as plastic counting bears or centimeter/gram cubes)
- Water in disposable or plastic bowls
- Paper towels, newspaper, and cloth towels
- Poster board, markers, tape, and plastic bags

Be Safe

Sponges should be large enough that they do not fit in mouths.

Getting Ready

Assemble a collection of dry sponges. Check that each fits in the balance. Create a chart to record children's results. Tape plastic bags on the chart in which children can display their sponges after the activity. (See photo.)

Student	Sponge		Number of Bears
		DRY	
		WET	
		DRY	
		WET	
		DRY	
		WET	
		DRY	
		WET	

Spotlight Vocabulary

- heavy
- light
- weight
- balance
- measure

Begin

1. Show a small group of children how to compare the weights of objects using a simple balance.

   Questions to guide the observing and comparing processes:

   > *What happens when you put objects in the balance pans?*

   > *How do you know if one object is heavier/lighter?*

   > *How do you know if the objects have the same weight?*

   Seen and heard:

   Children said, "It balances" and "Yellow and green bears weigh the same."

Continue

2. Have children work in pairs, with up to two pairs working at the same time. Ask each pair of children to use the balance to measure the weight of a dry sponge. Have children count the number of objects used to measure the sponge's weight. Ask children to record the results on the chart. (You may want to fill out the chart for younger children.)

Questions to guide the inquiry process:

> *How many objects did you need to match the dry sponge's weight?*

> *Do all dry sponges weigh the same?*

Seen and heard:

Children said, "He put too many bears in," "What if we take another out?" and "Mine weighs a hundred."

3. If the children have not completed **Advanced Inquiry 1: How Much Water?**, introduce the concept of a full sponge as discussed in step 1 of that activity. Have the children fill their sponges with water and weigh them again. Then, have the children squeeze the water out of the sponges, place them in the plastic bag on the chart, and record the results. Discuss results with the small group.

Questions to guide the observing and comparing processes:

> *Is a sponge heavier when it is dry or when it is wet? How do you know?*

> *Why would dry sponges and wet sponges have different weights?*

> *Do all wet sponges weigh the same?*

Seen and heard:

Children said, "It's heavier when wet" and "This sponge is bigger and weighs more."

4. Once all the children have had a chance to complete the activity and add their information to the chart, meet as a class to review and discuss the results. Ask children to compare dry and wet sponges, different-sized sponges, and different types of sponges (sea sponges versus man-made sponges).

5. Give children the opportunity to continue this investigation on their own.

   Questions to guide the investigation:
   > *What do you wonder about sponges and their weights?*
   > *How could you find out?*
   > *What did you do to find out?*
   > *What happened?*
   > *Do you wonder about anything else now?*

What to Look For

Look for the strategies that children use to organize their testing of materials. How do they keep track of how much each sponge weighs? How can they explain the differences between dry and wet sponges (using objects to show their weight)?

What connections do the children make about estimating the weights of sponges and objects? Do the children work with materials in a random or methodical way? How persistent are they in finding out more about sponges? How many tests are they willing to try?

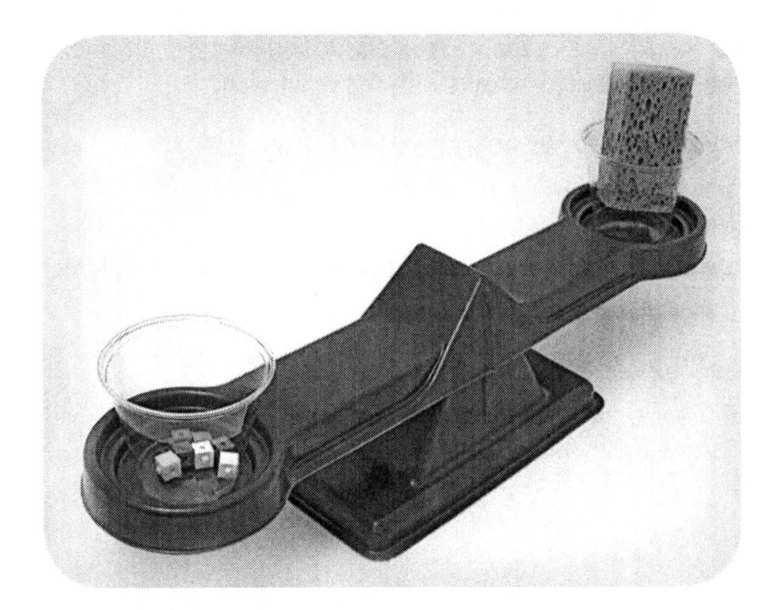

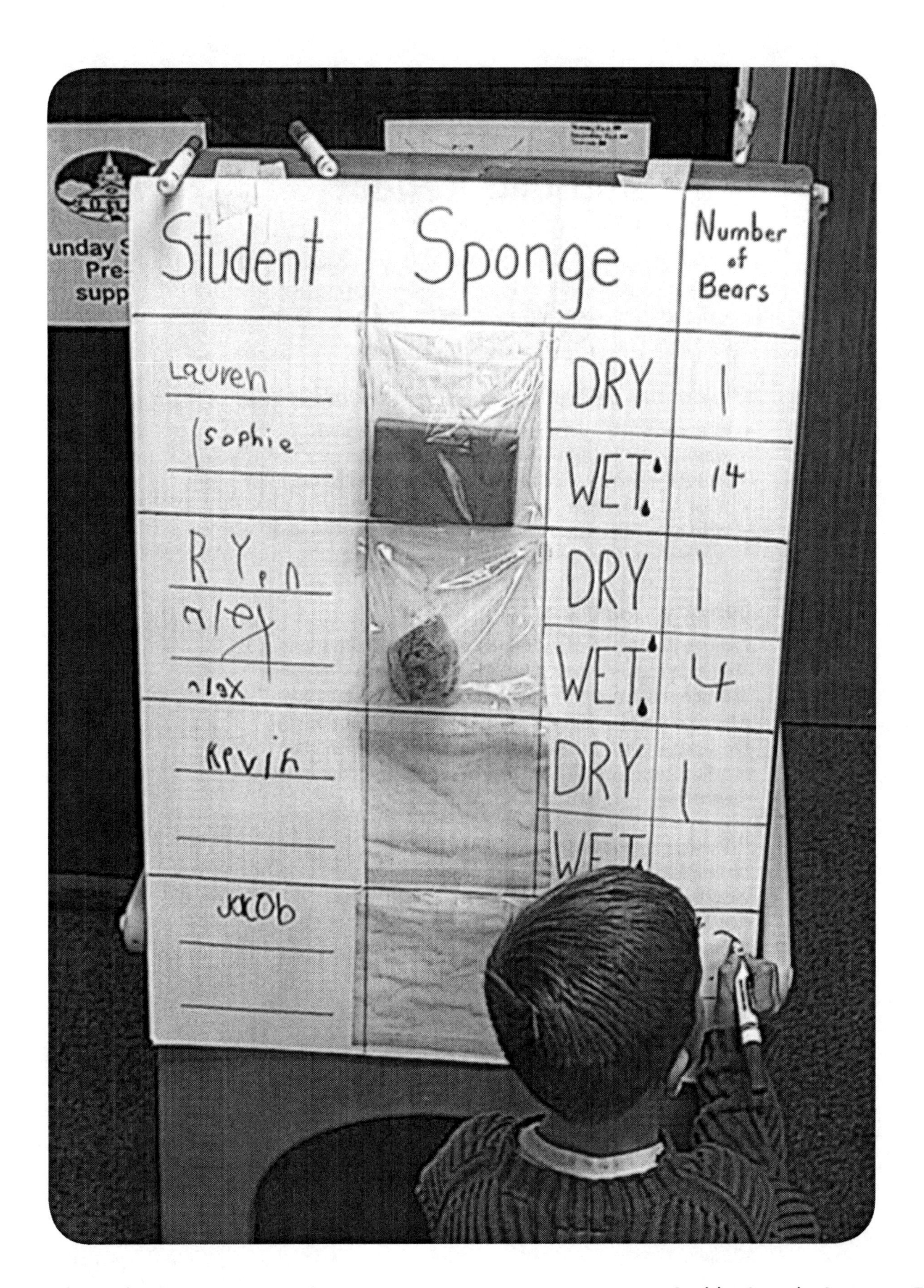
Student
Sponge
Number of Bears
Lauren
Sophie
DRY
1
WET
14
alex
DRY
1
WET
4
kevin
DRY
1
WET
Jacob

Stop and Reflect

After investigating how much water sponges can soak up, review with children what they have discovered so far. Keep a record of the children's ideas to show the progress of their learning.

Guide the reflection process by asking

- What can you tell people about sponges and water?
- What new things did you discover in your work?
- How did you know what happened? Were there any surprises?
- What did you notice?
- What else about sponges would you like to know and find out? How could you do that?

What to look for

Children have now had a variety of experiences with sponges. They have explored the materials both with teacher guidance and independently. During reflection, listen for details that tell about their experiences. Some children may focus on the processes they used to explore the sponges. Other children may focus on the results and their observations of the sponges themselves.

Encourage children to be descriptive and offer ideas to explain what they have learned.

Part 5:
Application

What is the application phase?

In the application phase, learners apply and use their understandings in new settings and situations. The activities in this phase can also serve as assessment tools.

During application, children

- use their learning in different ways,
- represent learning in various ways,
- apply learning to new situations, and
- formulate new hypotheses and repeat the learning cycle.

The teacher's role is to

- create links for application in the world outside the classroom,
- help children apply learning to new situations, and
- provide meaningful situations in which children use what they have learned.

Application 1:

Spongy Cakes

Children apply what they've learned about sponges when comparing sponges to cake.

Duration

1 small group session

Purpose

- Compare and contrast cake and sponges
- Observe the ability of cake to absorb liquid

What You Need

- Sponge cake dessert cups (such as Dolly Madison® Short Cakes) or sponge snack cakes (such as Hostess® Twinkies®)
- Plates, cups, and spoons
- Colored fruit juice
- Assortment of sponges used in previous investigations
- Magnifying lens

Be Safe

When comparing cake and sponges, be sure to point out to the children that we can eat cake but we can't eat sponges. Have children wash their hands before touching food.

Spotlight Vocabulary

- compare
- holes
- soak
- liquid

Begin

1. Show a small group of children a sponge cake dessert cup or snack cake and ask them if they think the cake will behave like a sponge and soak up liquid. Discuss with the children possible liquids that could be used to see if the cake acts like a sponge. Introduce the juice to be used in step 3 by telling the children what it is and why you selected it.

   Question to guide interest and enthusiasm:

   > *What could we do to test our cake to see if it behaves like a sponge?*

   Seen and heard:

   Children said, "Push on it" and "Wash the table with it!"

Continue

2. Give each child a piece of the cake on a plate and a sponge. Ask children to compare the two by using their senses. Have them break off a piece of cake and look at the texture. Have them take a closer look with a magnifying lens.

   Questions to guide interest and enthusiasm:

   > *How are the cake and the sponge the same?*

   > *How are the cake and the sponge different?*

3. Give each child a cup with a small amount of juice in it. Have each child pour the juice slowly onto the plate to see if the cake soaks up the juice. Observe and discuss what happens, then let the children eat the cake as a snack.

Questions to guide interest and enthusiasm:

> *What happened to the cake?*

> *What happened to the fruit juice?*

> *How is this cake like a sponge?*

> *How is this cake not like a sponge?*

Helpful Hint

Doing this activity in small groups helps the teacher record the children's ideas while they enjoy the snack.

What to Look For

Children can explain what they have learned about sponges by comparing the sponge cake to the real sponge. Encourage them to use descriptive words and details that reflect what they learned in previous activities. Listen for them to include Spotlight Vocabulary words in their discussion. Look for examples children may highlight as they explain their ideas.

Application 2:

Is This a Sponge?

Children apply what they've learned about sponges when comparing the properties of sponges and loofahs.

Duration

2 small group sessions and 1 large group session

Purpose

- Compare properties of sponges and loofahs
- Use observations to decide if loofahs are sponges

What You Need

- Several loofahs (These are actually dried squash, popular for rubbing off rough skin while bathing. They are sold with bath supplies.)
- I Wonder Data Sheet for each child (**Inquiry 4: I Wonder...** includes a sample data sheet on page 60.)
- Assortment of materials to test the loofahs (such as water, containers, paint, and paper)
- Assortment of sponges used in the previous investigations

Be Safe

Sponges and loofahs should be large enough that they do not fit in mouths.

Spotlight Vocabulary

- living
- animal
- plant
- squash

Begin

1. Working in small groups, challenge the children by presenting a loofah and asking, "Is this a sponge?" Let the children observe the loofah and compare it to what they previously learned about sponges.

   Questions to guide interest and enthusiasm:

   > *Have you ever seen these objects before?*

   > *What do you notice about them?*

   > *What are some things you have discovered about sponges?*

   > *How are these objects the same as sponges you've already seen? How are they different?*

2. The children will need to decide what experiments to carry out to find out if loofahs are sponges. Help them use I Wonder Data Sheets from **Inquiry 4: I Wonder...** to record what they want to do for their investigations. For example, the children may wish to explore the holes of the loofahs and print with them using paint (as in **Inquiry 3: Printing Holes**) or experiment with loofahs at the water table.

   Questions to guide interest and enthusiasm:

   > *What could you do to find out more?*

   > *What materials would you need for your investigations?*

   Seen and heard:

   Children said, "Put it in the water."

Continue

3. Let the children do the experiments they have planned with loofahs and compare results to their work with sponges. Have the children summarize their findings on the I Wonder Data Sheets.

   Questions to guide interest and enthusiasm:

   > *What experiments did you try with the loofahs?*

   > *If you used water or paint, what happened when you tested the loofahs with these? How did the results compare?*

   Seen and heard:

   Children said, "I put it in the water," "It's hard," and "They have big holes."

4. Ask the children to show their I Wonder Data Sheets to the class and share their findings.

5. Remind the children that sea sponges come from animals. Point out that loofahs come from plants; when they grow, they have an outer skin and seeds like a squash. (Show the loofah plant pictured in this activity.) Sponges and loofahs are both living things. They both have holes, but loofahs are not good at soaking up liquids, which is an important function of sponges.

Question to guide interest and enthusiasm:

> *What are some important things to remember about sponges?*

What to Look For

Listen to the children as they seek to answer the questions about loofahs being sponges. Encourage them to apply what they learned about sponges in designing experiments to compare the loofahs to the sponges. Listen for the children to include Spotlight Vocabulary words in their discussion. Encourage the children to use details and actual observations to explain their answers.

Stop and Reflect

What you need

- small pieces of paper
- pencils and crayons
- large sheet of paper

Reflection activity

Give each child a small piece of paper. Ask the children to draw or write something that they have learned from the investigations.

Bring the children together to show their papers and share their discoveries with the class. You may want to sort the papers into categories as children share. For example, one category could be sea sponges and the other, man-made sponges. Children can help you decide which category each paper belongs with. Use a large sheet of paper, and post the children's sheets as they share their ideas. When all have shared, display this data in the room.

Part 6: Sponges Across the Curriculum

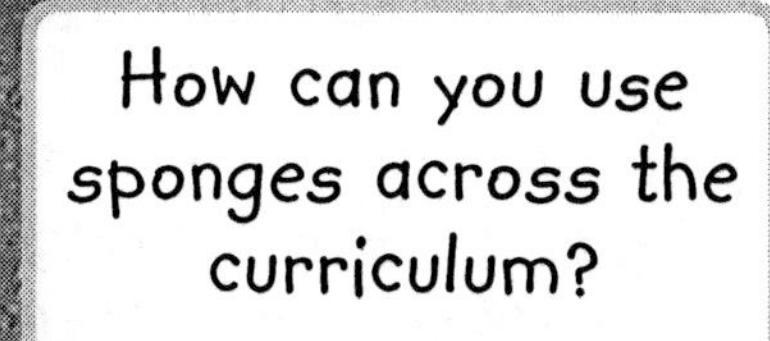

How can you use sponges across the curriculum?

This section includes fun ideas for extending children's learning with sponges into dramatic play, writing, art, biology, and cooking.

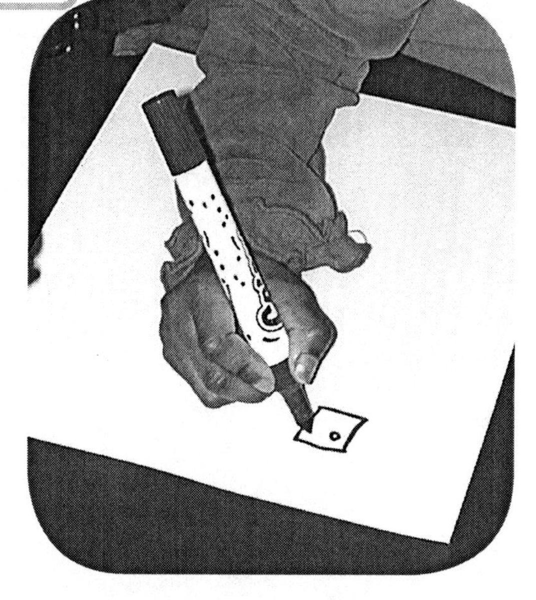

Across the Curriculum 1:

Creative Dramatics

Children build sponge tunnels and pretend to be animals living in the ocean.

Duration

1 large group session, plus optional open play sessions

Purpose

- Understand more about sponges as living creatures
- Experience the habitat of a sponge

What You Need

- *Sponges Are Skeletons,* by Barbara Juster Esbensen, or similar resource
- Optional: *Origins*, the first part of an eight-episode film series called *The Shape of Life*

  This film is available from PBS; http://www.shop.pbs.org.
- Music to help children imagine they are underwater

  Many types of nature music are available. Handel's Water Music *is a classical favorite.*
- Materials to build play tunnels (such as chairs, tables, sheets, towels, and blankets, or commercial play tunnels)

Getting Ready

Make a giant sponge model by building tunnels for children to crawl under and through. Cover chairs and tables with sheets, towels, and blankets. As an alternative, set up commercial play tunnels.

Spotlight Vocabulary

- skeleton
- food
- pores
- underwater
- habitat
- tunnel

Begin

1. Remind children that sea sponges are animals. To help children visualize sponges and other life in the ocean, read pages 16–17 of *Sponges Are Skeletons* (or a similar resource) and show the pictures of sponges in Part 8: All About Sponges of this book.

   Questions to guide children's thinking:
   > *Where do sponges live?*
   > *What else lives in the ocean?*

2. Ask children to imagine that their classroom is an ocean.

   Question to guide children's thinking:
   > *What plants and animals do you imagine seeing?*

3. Read pages 12–15 of *Sponges Are Skeletons* (or a similar resource) to the children to review the idea that sponges take in water and food through the holes and tunnels in their body. You may wish to show a short excerpt from *Origins* (see What You Need) that shows scientists demonstrating how sponges pump water to feed.

4. Tell children that you have made a giant sponge for their ocean. Show them the tunnels in the sponge, and explain that they will pretend to be small sea creatures that swim inside sponges. The children could be small fish, shrimp, or even tiny plankton that a sponge would like to eat.

Helpful Hint

While the music is playing, you can use a "magic" wand to tap children and change them into animals.

Continue

5. Play a short selection of music and have the children pretend to be small animals in the sea. Have the children start moving in their own space. Slowly have them begin to move around the room. Explain that this is the place where sponges live—their habitat.

6. Send the children through the play sponge tunnels. For safety, limit the number of children in each tunnel and monitor the children's movement in and out of the tunnels.

7. Children can repeat the activity several times with different lengths and kinds of tunnels. The tunnels could also be left assembled for open play period explorations.

8. Have the children describe what they experienced while pretending to move through a sponge.

What to Look For

In the discussion about sponges, listen for children to tell about their experiences using descriptive words. Encourage them to provide details using Spotlight Vocabulary words.

Across the Curriculum 2:
Writing to Learn

Children share their thoughts and knowledge about sponges with their teacher, classmates, and families by creating stories that summarize what they learned through observation, exploration, and investigation.

Duration

1 small group session and 1 large group session

Purpose

- Document ideas about sponges as living creatures
- Write stories about sponges
- Create pictures to tell about sponges

What You Need

- Optional: examples of children's work completed during the unit
- Paper and illustration tools for children to create pictures
- Optional: digital camera and printer or instant camera

Spotlight Vocabulary

Encourage children to use the Spotlight Vocabulary from different activities they have done.

Begin

1. Meet with the children in small groups to improve participation and individual contributions. Ask children what they learned about sponges. Each child should be encouraged to contribute. You can display samples of their previous work to help children with ideas.

2. Have each child draw a picture showing something he or she learned about sponges.

3. Have children dictate stories based on their pictures. You may have several children contribute to a longer story or individual children telling their own stories. Encourage children to use the Spotlight Vocabulary from different activities they have done. If available, a digital camera and printer or an instant camera can allow you to quickly add pictures of children and sponges to the book.

4. Assemble the pictures and stories into a class book. Remember to include children's names as authors and to create a title.

Continue

5. Read the class book aloud to the class. Highlight children's illustrations and contributions.

> **Helpful Hint**
>
> Make copies of the story for each child to take home. This empowers children to see the results of their work and to share their ideas just like scientists do. It also provides a valuable learning link between your classroom and home.

What to Look For

Watch for children to describe what they learned working with sponges. Listen for them to include Spotlight Vocabulary words in their contribution to the story. Encourage the children to recall details from their work and experiences with sponges.

Across the Curriculum 3:
Sponge Painting

Now that the children have learned about different types of sponges, the experience of painting with sponges will take on new dimensions.

Duration

Several small group sessions

Purpose

- Learn techniques of sponge painting
- Create pieces of art

What You Need

- Sponges
- Various types of paper
- Tempera paint
- Watercolor paint
- Acrylic paint (for use on clay flower pots)
- Items to decorate with sponge painting (such as clay flower pots or small cardboard boxes)
- Samples of spongeware pottery or other items decorated by sponge painting (See photos.)
- Optional: music

Be Safe

Remind children not to put sponges in their mouths.

Spotlight Vocabulary

- paint
- mix

Begin

1. Explain that artists use sponges to mix colors and to paint. Show children examples of sponge paintings.

2. Provide children with sponges, tempera paint, and paper. Encourage them to experiment with different types of sponges and colors on different types of paper. Music during painting is an excellent addition.

Continue

3. Explain that sponges are used in watercolor painting to take color off the paper and create effects, such as white clouds in a blue sky. Demonstrate the following technique and then have the children try it: Cover a sheet of heavy paper with watercolor paint. While the paint is still wet, use a damp sponge to lift paint off the paper in patterns. (The amount of color removed depends on the type of paper and colors of paint used.)

4. Show children examples of spongeware pottery or other items decorated with sponge painting. Invite children to use sponge painting to decorate items such as clay flower pots or small cardboard boxes available at craft stores.

5. Have the children share their work with the group and explain how they used sponges to make art. Record each child's explanation. Display the artwork along with the children's descriptions of what they did. Such a display shows children the value of art and their work.

What to Look For

Look for children to mimic sponge painting techniques and make creative art pieces. Listen for detailed, descriptive words as children explain how they used sponges to produce their artwork.

Across the Curriculum 4:

Sponges and Seeds

Children learn that water in sponges can help seeds grow.

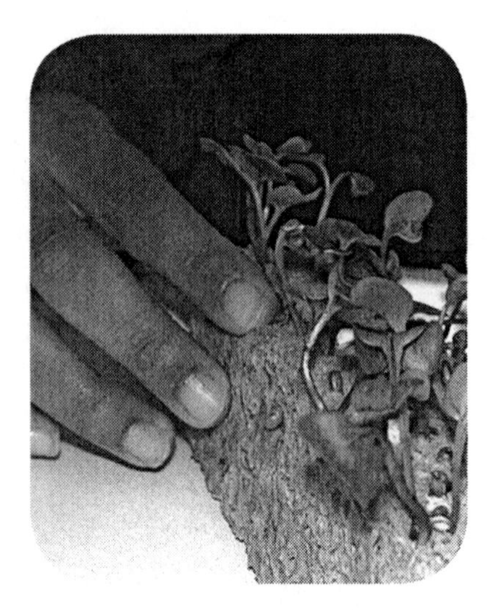

Duration

Several large group sessions

Purpose

- Observe how moisture in sponges can help make seeds grow

What You Need

- Flat, man-made sponges
- Water
- Plates
- Marker, pencil, or pen
- Seeds that germinate quickly (such as radish, grass, mustard, or mixed birdseed)
- Surface near a window

Be Safe

Remind children not to put sponges in their mouths.

Spotlight Vocabulary

- seed
- sprout

Begin

1. Explain that seeds need water to grow into baby plants. Show children sponges and a packet of seeds. Ask children how they think sponges can be used to help the seeds grow.

2. Have children watch as you set up sponges and seeds for the class to observe. You may want to have children work in small groups to set up wet sponges of their own.

    a. Soak one sponge in water. Squeeze out the excess water until the sponge is just moist. Put the sponge on a plate that is labeled "wet."

    b. Put a dry sponge on another plate that is labeled "dry."

c. Open a package of seeds. Carefully put some seeds into the holes of both sponges. Put the plates on a flat surface near a window.

Continue

3. Keep the sponges labeled "wet" moist. Have the children watch what happens for the next few weeks.

4. Ask the children to compare the results achieved with the dry sponge to those achieved with the wet sponge and draw or write what they observed. Ask them to explain why some seeds grew and others didn't.

What to Look For

Look for children to demonstrate, through verbal descriptions and drawings, their awareness that sponges can hold water and help seeds grow.

Across the Curriculum 5:

Sponge Cooking

Add cooking to the classroom by making baked goods that resemble sponges.

Duration

Several large group sessions

Purpose

- Measure ingredients in a recipe
- Participate in a group project
- Compare baked items to sponges

What You Need

- Ingredients to make sponge cake or injera (Ethiopian flat bread) as called for in the recipes at the end of this activity
- Baking equipment (as called for in the recipes at the end of this activity)
- Tasty liquids to test with the foods (such as milk or juice to test with the cake and stew or gravy to test with the injera)
- Assortment of sponges

Be Safe

Keep electric mixers and hot ingredients away from children. Keep children away from hot burners and ovens. Have children wash their hands before touching food. When comparing cake and sponges, be sure to point out to the children that we can eat cake but we can't eat sponges.

Spotlight Vocabulary

- stir
- compare
- measure
- holes
- same
- different

Begin

1. Have children help you prepare sponge cake or injera. If you choose to make injera, explain how it is used: In Ethiopia, injera is used as both a plate and a spoon. Injera is placed on a large tray, and stews are spooned on top. People use other pieces of injera to scoop up and eat the stews.

Continue

2. Tell children that the secret to sponge-type cakes and breads is the gas bubbles that create holes in the batter as it rises and cooks. Ask children to look for the holes in the sponge-type foods you made. Give the children sponges to compare to the foods.

   Questions to guide the observing and comparing processes:
   > *How are the foods you made similar to sponges?*
   > *How are the foods different than sponges?*

3. Have children experiment to see if the sponge-type foods will soak up liquid.

   Questions to guide the observing process:
   > *What happened to the food?*
   > *What happened to the liquid?*
   > *Can you describe how they taste?*

4. Serve the baked items for a snack.

What to Look For

When comparing sponges and baked goods, watch for children to compare physical traits, such as holes, absorbency, color, and shape. Encourage children to use all of their senses during the comparison (but don't let them taste the sponge).

Sponge Cake

Sponge cake is a type of cake called a foam cake. The foam from beaten egg whites provides the leavening rather than baking soda or powder.

Ingredients

- 5 eggs, separated
- 1 tablespoon lemon juice
- 1 cup sugar (split into ¾ cup and ¼ cup)
- ¼ teaspoon salt
- 1 cup cake flour
- Optional: confectioners' sugar or frosting

Directions

1. Preheat oven to 325°F.
2. Line bottom of 9-inch tube pan or two 8-inch round cake pans with wax paper. (Trace bottom of pan on wax paper and cut out paper to fit in pan.)
3. Separate the eggs and set the egg whites aside. Beat the egg yolks with lemon juice until pale and thick. Gradually add ¾ cup sugar and beat thoroughly.
4. In a separate bowl, beat egg whites until foamy. Add salt and continue beating until whites hold soft peaks. Slowly add remaining ¼ cup sugar. Beat until stiff but not dry.
5. Stir about ¼ of the beaten whites into the egg yolk mixture.
6. Spoon the remaining whites over the yolk mixture and sift the flour on top. Gently fold until blended. Spoon into pans.
7. Bake 45–55 minutes for tube pan and 25–30 minutes for layer pans, or until toothpick or straw comes out clean.
8. Invert pan on rack and let cool completely.
9. Remove from pan. Dust with confectioners' sugar or frost, if desired.

Quick Injera

Traditional injera is made from a tiny grain called teff. Because teff can be hard to find, this recipe uses wheat flour. The injera batter is usually allowed to ferment for several days to give it a sourdough-like flavor. This quick version is cooked right away. Injera is cooked only on one side, and the bottom should be not get brown.

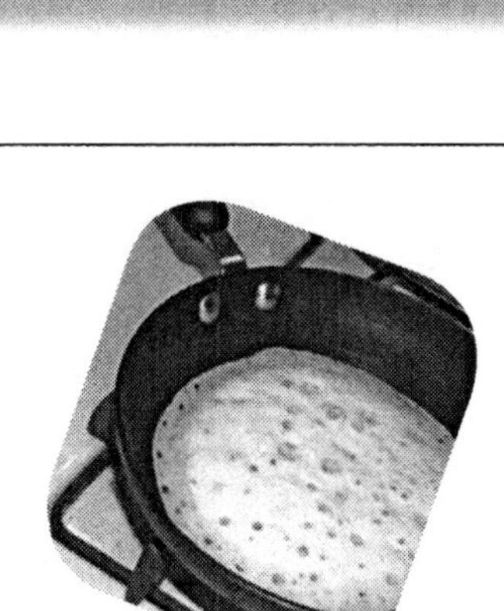

Ingredients

- 2 cups self-rising flour
- 2 cups seltzer or bubbly water

Directions

1. Mix the flour with the water for a somewhat liquid consistency.
2. Heat a nonstick 9-inch skillet. The secret of making injera is to get the pan very hot. The pan is ready when a drop of water bounces on its surface.
3. Pour about ⅓ cup of the batter in the skillet all at once. Swirl the pan so that the entire bottom is evenly coated, then return to heat.
4. When the moisture has evaporated and lots of "holes" appear on the surface, remove the injera with a spatula. Let each injera cool and then stack them as you go along.
5. If the first injera is undercooked, try using less of the mixture, perhaps ¼ cup, and maybe cook it a bit longer. Be sure not to overcook it. Injera should be soft and pliable so that it can be rolled or folded, like a crepe.

Part 7: Science for Young Learners

How can preschool children be taught science?

This section contains information on developmentally appropriate science instruction for young children, including fundamental concepts and process skills, inquiry-based science, teaching with learning cycles, and documenting children's learning.

Why Preschool Science?

Process Skill Power

"Concepts are the building blocks of knowledge; they allow people to organize and categorize information. During early childhood, children actively engage in acquiring fundamental concepts and in learning fundamental process skills."

Karen Lind, 1999

Why bother with science in preschool? Young children can't memorize the geologic periods or understand chemical reactions. Learning ABCs and how to share, listen, and even tie shoes, is a challenging business! Plus, the school day is too short to accomplish all we have to do now. Why not wait until children are older to introduce science?

The National Science Education Standards emphasize that all children can learn science and that all children should have the opportunity to become scientifically literate. In *Science in Early Childhood: Developing and Acquiring Fundamental Concepts and Skills,* Karen Lind writes "In order for this learning to happen, the effort to introduce children to the essential experiences of science inquiry and explorations must begin at an early age." (Lind, 1999)

Reaching Potentials: Transforming Early Childhood Curriculum and Assessment (from the National Association for the Education of Young Children) summarizes what developmentally-appropriate science instruction for young children is...and is not. The authors use the term "sciencing" to convey the child's active involvement in learning about science and to emphasize process in effective science teaching.

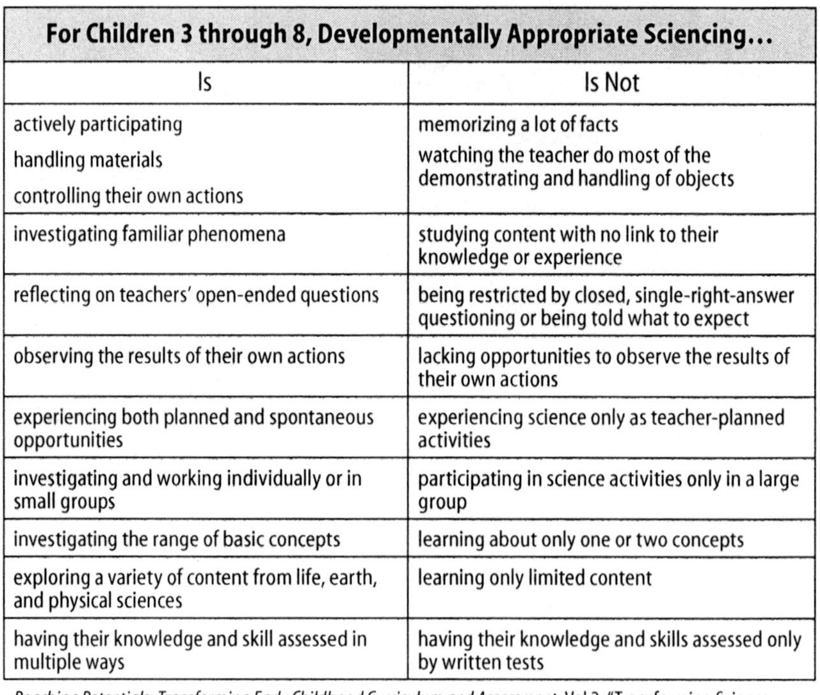

For Children 3 through 8, Developmentally Appropriate Sciencing...

Is	Is Not
actively participating handling materials controlling their own actions	memorizing a lot of facts watching the teacher do most of the demonstrating and handling of objects
investigating familiar phenomena	studying content with no link to their knowledge or experience
reflecting on teachers' open-ended questions	being restricted by closed, single-right-answer questioning or being told what to expect
observing the results of their own actions	lacking opportunities to observe the results of their own actions
experiencing both planned and spontaneous opportunities	experiencing science only as teacher-planned activities
investigating and working individually or in small groups	participating in science activities only in a large group
investigating the range of basic concepts	learning about only one or two concepts
exploring a variety of content from life, earth, and physical sciences	learning only limited content
having their knowledge and skill assessed in multiple ways	having their knowledge and skills assessed only by written tests

Reaching Potentials: Transforming Early Childhood Curriculum and Assessment, Vol 2. "Transforming Science Curriculum," 1995, S. Kilmer and H. Hofman, pg. 62. Reproduced with permission of the National Association for the Education of Young Children.

When presented in a way that is meaningful for young minds, preschool science education provides the foundation for a lifetime of science learning both in and out of school. The goal of the *Big Science for Little Hands* series is to help preschool children develop an understanding of **fundamental concepts about the physical world** and the **fundamental process skills** suitable for their developmental level.

Fundamental Concepts

The fundamental concepts allow children to organize their experiences with the physical world into meaningful patterns—the beginning of true science learning. How do children develop an awareness of these fundamental concepts? They need repeated, personal experiences with materials and events from their everyday world and the tools—in the form of process skills—to help them make sense of these experiences and the world around them.

The activities in this book provide a specific progression of experiences that help children build an understanding of the fundamental concepts listed below. This progression is in the form of a learning cycle. (See page 110 for a discussion of learning cycles.)

Process Skill Power

"Although young children are not methodical, they naturally use one or more [process skills] as they investigate everything that attracts their attention. The early childhood teacher's job is to increase awareness and use of these skills."

Sally Kilmer and Helenmarie Hofman, 1995

Fundamental Concepts	
Fundamental concepts about the physical world for the preschool level	Examples of use in activities
Objects and events have observable characteristics.	In **Exploration 1: A Closer Look at Sponges,** children learn that objects have observable characteristics as they explore sponges with their senses of touch, smell, hearing, and sight.
A person can act on objects or materials to change them and observe the results of their action.	In **Exploration 4: Sponges Get Wet,** children find that their actions, dipping sponges in water, can change the sponges by making them wet, heavier, and sometimes larger. Another action, squeezing the water out, changes the sponges again.
The physical world has patterns that help a person predict what will happen next.	By the time they reach **Application 1: Spongy Cakes,** children have observed patterns of events that help them predict what will happen when a spongelike material (sponge cake) is placed in juice.

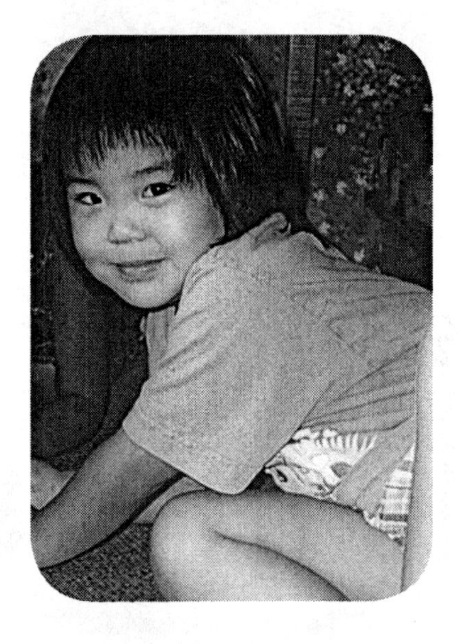

Fundamental Process Skills

Each activity in this book helps children develop one or more of the process skills appropriate for the preschool level. How we define these process skills is important, because what one person understands to be "measuring" or "organizing" may not be developmentally appropriate for this level. Review the following list and definitions carefully. Note that preschool children can begin practicing simpler versions of intermediate-level process skills.

Process Skill Power

"Children at all ages can be successful at inquiry."

Doris Ash, Cappy Greene, and Marilyn Austin, 2000

Process Skills	
Fundamental process skills for the preschool level	
Observing	Using the senses to gather information about objects or events is the most fundamental of the scientific thinking processes. Rich observation experiences enable children to create a repertoire of possible properties that make up objects or events and form a foundation for comparing and organizing.
Communicating	Sharing oral or written ideas and descriptions in a way that helps others understand the meaning.
Comparing	Examining the character of objects in order to discover similarities or differences. Comparing builds upon the process of observing and begins in younger children with comparing two objects at a time.
Measuring	Comparing objects to arbitrary units that may or may not be standardized. Measuring skills begin to develop as children compare objects to one another (such as bigger/smaller, hotter/colder). The skill then extends to comparing objects to nonstandard units of measure (such as one block equals three counting bears). Beginning in primary grades, children can understand the value of using standard units such as pounds and inches.
Organizing	This skill includes grouping, classifying, seriating (ordering objects along a continuum), and sequencing (placing events one after another so that they tell a logical story). • Grouping begins at about age 3 with resemblance sorting: putting objects together (in pairs, piles, or chains) on the basis of one-to-one correspondence. Each pair or pile may be based on a different kind of resemblance, such as red objects in one pile and square ones in another. • Consistent and exhaustive sorting starts at about age 6, when a child will use up all the pieces in a set using one consistent rule for grouping, such as color. • Multiple membership classifying—the ability to place an object into more than one category at the same time or into one category based on two or more simultaneous properties—begins at about age 8.
Simple versions of intermediate process skills for preschool children	
Reasonable guessing	More than a simple guess, based on prior knowledge. For example, perceiving a pattern emerging and surmising how it will continue. Reasonable guessing is a step towards predicting.
Early data collecting and interpreting	Can include counting and making pictures to represent information discovered by exploration. Children can reflect upon these results together. Teachers can model these process skills with the children as ways to organize information found in exploration and investigation. This skill gives purpose to activities and further experiments.

Facilitating "Sciencing"

Spontaneous sciencing occurs every day. Whenever children see something of interest, wonder about it, and investigate to answer their questions, sciencing is going on. These experiences are certainly valuable, but "what children gain can be enhanced and increased by planning. Both the classroom environment and our teaching strategies should encourage active sciencing." (Kilmer, 1995)

Teachers are the role models and facilitators of sciencing. As models, teachers need to display all of the behaviors identified as outcomes for the children. "Teachers are not expected to know all there is to know about sciencing. What is important is that the teacher be open, enthusiastic, and willing to wonder 'What happens if…?'" (Kilmer, 1995)

Science learning flourishes when teachers facilitate a classroom atmosphere that respects each child's contribution, supports inquiry and experimentation without passing judgements about right and wrong, and embraces "mistakes" as opportunities for new discoveries. Strategic comments and questions can focus and extend children's thinking. By carefully observing a child's behavior, teachers can put into words the unspoken question the child seems to be thinking about.

One effective technique for helping children try new approaches to investigations is to join the child in their activity and begin by imitating what the child is doing. The adult then gradually adds something new to his or her actions. "If, for instance, the focus is on bubbles, after the child has had time to explore blowing bubbles in various ways but has not spontaneously used some of the different bubble-makers provided, the teacher sits beside the child. After using the same bubble-maker as the child is using, the teacher begins to try different ones." (Kilmer, 1995) Frequently, the child will notice the teacher's behavior and expand his or her own exploration.

Process Skill Power

"Children who have many interesting, direct experiences over time with science concepts will gradually understand the broader principles as they develop the cognitive skills to make more abstract generalizations."

Sally Kilmer and Helenmarie Hofman, 1995

Self-Directed Inquiry

As children develop and practice the process skills and inquiry modeled by the teacher, their ability to initiate, plan, and conduct self-directed inquiry grows. Children "begin the process of asking and answering their own questions, which is at the heart of the inquiry experience." (Villavicencio, 2000)

Joanna Villavicencio's experiences doing self-directed inquiry with 4- and 5-year-old children shows the ability of young children to benefit from these opportunities. As children explore, she guides them to follow a five-part structure that helps organize their investigations:

- form a question;
- make a plan;
- do the investigation;
- record and report; and
- reflect, revisit, and plan again.

Until they have experience with inquiry, children often have difficulty asking questions that can be tested. Teachers need to actively facilitate children's efforts to ask such questions. Wendy Cheong writes, "While watching the children explore, I encourage them to ask questions about whatever seems curious to them....I support them in various ways. For example, I model techniques and ask a lot of open-ended questions, such as: "Can you tell me what you are trying to find out with this instrument?" Eventually, the children get used to hearing the kinds of questions that can lead to investigations." (Cheong, 2000)

Jane Bresnik models this process by asking questions that begin with "I wonder," such as "I wonder what will happen if I hold the ramp higher?" The words "I wonder..." become the first part of a template Jane uses to help children organize their investigations. Children state their "I wonder" question, explain their plan, conduct their tests, and then explain what happened using the "I found out..." prompt. (Bresnik, 2000)

As children begin their investigations, teachers need to work with them by observing, questioning, supporting their efforts, and redirecting their investigations. Reporting the results of investigations to others is an important step. Joanna Villavicencio explains that "In the beginning, the children have a hard time articulating their discoveries, so I help them find the right words to explain what they discovered.... I have seen how language develops during the inquiry process. As children share what they see, they find words to express and refine their thinking." (Villavicencio, 2000)

How Children Learn

Current research on how humans learn is helping educators understand what fosters learning and how to improve ineffective or even detrimental aspects of teaching. In "How New Science Curriculums Reflect Brain Research," Lawrence Lowery describes a view of learning based on research in the cognitive sciences:

- learners construct understanding for themselves,
- to understand is to know relationships, and
- knowing relationships depends on having prior knowledge.

The brain needs data it can use to construct knowledge. Our senses are like windows that allow the brain to collect and store data with everything we do, perceive, think, or feel. "Learners do not simply mirror what they are told or what they read. The brain does not store a picture of an event. It does not directly record anything that is shown." (Lowery, 1998) What the brain does do is store information clustered into different areas of the brain with networks of pathways connecting these places. For example, sensory perceptions are grouped in different places in the brain—shapes, colors, movements, textures, and aromas are each stored in their own places. Components of language are also stored in their own places—nouns in one place, verbs in another.

"As the brain constructs connections among brain cells, it connects the organization of words, objects, events, and relationships. . .The result is that human knowledge is stored in clusters and organized within the brain into systems that people use to interpret familiar situations and reason about new ones." (Lowery, 1998) The more avenues that children have to receive data through the senses, the more connections their brain will make.

Knowledge is constructed through experience, but the quality of that construction is greatly affected by how well the brain organizes and stores relationships. For example, a child exploring a magnet experiences the following relationships:

- a relationship between the learner and the object (how the hand and arm are positioned to hold the magnet);
- cause and effect relationships between the learner's actions and observed results (how the magnet can be moved and manipulated); and
- cause and effect relationships in an interaction between objects in the environment (how other objects behave in the presence of the magnet).

As exploration continues, "learners try to link new perceptions to what they have already constructed in the brain's storage systems. They use this prior knowledge to interpret the new material in terms of established knowledge." (Lowery, 1998) Bits of information that are isolated from integration with prior knowledge are forgotten. The more opportunities children have to explore relationships among objects and ideas and to use their prior knowledge, the richer and more permanent their constructions of knowledge will be. This is accomplished through rehearsals—reinforcing what has been learned while adding something new.

Find Out More

Bredekamp, Sue, and Teresa Rosegrant, eds. ***Reaching Potentials: Appropriate Curriculum and Assessment for Young Children.*** Vol. 1. Washington, DC: National Association for the Education of Young Children (NAEYC), 1992.

Connect: Inquiry Learning Issue Vol. 13(4), 2000: pgs. 1–26.

Lind, Karen. ***Exploring Science in Early Childhood: A Developmental Approach.*** Albany, NY: Delmar Publishers, 2000.

Lowery, Lawrence. "**How New Science Curriculums Reflect Brain Research.**" *Educational Leadership* Vol. 56(3), 1998: pgs. 26–30.

Lowery, Lawrence. ***The Scientific Thinking Process.*** Berkeley, CA: Lawrence Hall of Science, 1992.

National Association for the Education of Young Children (NAEYC). ***Developmentally Appropriate Practice in Early Childhood Programs Serving Children from Birth through Age 8.*** 1997. Available: http://www.naeyc.org/resources/position_statements/daptoc.htm. April 25, 2003.

National Research Council. ***National Science Education Standards: Observe, Interact, Change, Learn.*** Washington, DC: National Academy Press, 1996.

Project 2061, ed. ***Dialogue on Early Childhood Science, Mathematics, and Technology Education.*** Washington, DC: American Association for the Advancement of Science (AAAS), 1999.

Good Science at Any Age

The list below was developed by teachers and administrators participating in the Vermont Elementary Science Project. They write, "The intent is not to use this guide as a checklist, but as a statement of what we value in the areas of science processes, science dispositions, and science concept development. We urge you to capture evidence of your own students engaging in these indicators."

Inquiry-Based Science: What Does It Look Like?

When students are doing inquiry based science, an observer will see that

Children view themselves as scientists in the process of learning.

- Children look forward to doing science.
- They demonstrate a desire to learn more.
- They seek to collaborate and work cooperatively with their peers.
- They are confident in doing science; they demonstrate a willingness to modify ideas, take risks, and display healthy skepticism.

Children accept an "invitation to learn" and readily engage in the exploration process.

- Children exhibit curiosity and ponder observations.
- They move around, selecting and using the materials they need.
- They take the opportunity and the time to try out their own ideas.

Children plan and carry out investigations.

- Children design a way to try out their ideas, not expecting to be told what to do.
- They plan ways to verify, extend, or discard ideas.
- They carry out investigations by handling materials, observing, measuring, and recording data.

Children communicate using a variety of methods.

- Children express ideas in a variety of ways, such as with journals, reporting, drawing, graphing, and charting.
- They listen, speak, and write about science with parents, teachers, and peers.
- They use the language of the processes of science.
- They communicate their level of understanding of concepts that they have developed to date.

Children propose explanations and solutions and build a store of concepts.

- Children offer explanations from a store of previous knowledge.
- They use investigations to answer their own questions.
- They sort information and decide what information is important.
- They are willing to revise explanations as they gain new knowledge.

Children raise questions.

- Children ask questions (verbally or through actions).
- They use questions to lead them to investigations that generate further questions or ideas.
- They value and enjoy asking questions as an important part of science.

Children use observation.

- Children observe, as opposed to just looking.
- They see details; they detect sequences and events; they notice changes, similarities, and differences.
- They make connections to previously held ideas.

Children critique their science practices.

- They use indicators to assess their own work.
- They report their strengths and weaknesses.
- They reflect with their peers.

The Vermont Elementary Science Project (VESP) is located at Trinity College, McAuley Hall, Burlington, VT 05401; (802) 658-3664. VESP is a grant awarded to The NETWORK, Inc., Andover, MA, by the National Science Foundation.

Teaching with Learning Cycles

What are learning cycles and why teach with them? A learning cycle is a structured approach to science teaching that takes into account what we know about how children learn. The work of researchers such as Piaget, Vygotsky, and Lowery has taught us that children acquire new concepts and skills by building upon what they already know and are able to do. This process is called the construction of knowledge.

In *Guidelines for Appropriate Curriculum Content and Assessment in Programs Serving Children Ages 3 through 8,* the National Association for the Education of Young Children (NAEYC) recommends that "the curriculum provides conceptual frameworks for children so that their mental constructions based on prior knowledge become more complex over time." (NAEYC, 1990)

Often, the early childhood science curriculum consists of conceptually unrelated activities chosen to coordinate with the seasons of the year or some other theme. NAEYC encourages science curriculum that builds conceptually upon itself rather than only coordinating with such a theme: "As in menu planning, the individual recipes may be appropriate and valuable, but without a framework and organization, they may fail to provide the opportunity for rich conceptual development that is likely with a more coherent, thoughtful approach."

Providing this "coherent, thoughtful approach" can be a challenge, but the structure of a learning cycle gives teachers a framework for doing so. In *How New Science Curriculums Reflect Brain Research,* Lawrence Lowery explains, "The learning cycle is viewed as a way to take students on a quest for knowledge that leads to the construction of knowledge. It is used both as a curriculum development procedure and a teaching strategy." A learning cycle creates a sequence of instructions that provides "a rehearsal of prior knowledge constructions, thus making them more permanent, and provides something new that the brain can assimilate into its prior construction, thus enriching and extending those constructions."

Typically, a learning cycle has four phases, each with one or more activities. The phases of the learning cycle are summarized on the following pages. This summary is adapted from NAEYC's *Guidelines for Appropriate Curriculum Content and Assessment for Programs Serving Children Ages 3 through 8.*

Process Skill Power

"The sequence of... instruction is important to move children from being novices to becoming experts. Each new challenge does two things: provides a rehearsal of prior knowledge constructions, thus making them more permanent, and provides something new that the brain can assimilate into its prior construction, thus enriching and extending those constructions."

Lawrence Lowery, 1998

Phase 1: Awareness—What's in my world? What do I know?

The awareness phase helps children develop broad recognition of the parameters of the learning—events, objects, people, or concepts.

During awareness, children

- experience,
- awaken curiosity, and
- develop an interest.

The teacher's role is to

- create a rich environment;
- provide opportunities by introducing new objects, people, events, or concepts;
- invite and encourage interest by posing a problem or question;
- respond to children's interest; and
- show interest and enthusiasm.

Phase 2: Exploration—What more can I find out about my world?

The exploration phase enables children to construct personal meaning through sensory experiences with objects, people, events, or concepts.

During exploration, children

- observe and explore materials,
- collect information, and
- construct their own understandings and meanings from their experiences.

The teacher's role is to

- facilitate, support, and enhance exploration;
- ask open-ended questions;
- respect children's thinking and rule systems;
- allow for constructive error; and
- model ways to organize information from experiences.

Phase 3: Inquiry—How can I research new things?

The inquiry phase of the learning cycle enables children to deepen and refine their understanding.

During inquiry, children

- examine,
- investigate,
- propose explanations,
- compare own thinking with that of others,
- generalize, and
- relate to prior learning.

The teacher's role is to

- help children refine understanding,
- ask more focused questions,
- provide information when requested, and
- help children make connections between prior experiences and their investigations.

Phase 4: Application—How can I apply what I learn?

In the application phase, learners apply and use their understandings in new settings and situations. The activities in this phase can also serve as assessment tools.

During application, children

- use their learning in different ways,
- represent learning in various ways,
- apply learning to new situations, and
- formulate new hypotheses and repeat learning cycle.

The teacher's role is to

- create links for application in the world outside the classroom,
- help children apply learning to new situations, and
- provide meaningful situations in which children use what they have learned.

Throughout the learning cycle, open-ended questions encourage the child to put into words what he or she is observing, doing, and wondering. When teaching with a learning cycle, teachers can ask focusing questions to support each phase of the learning cycle.

Find Out More

Barman, Charles R. "**Teaching Teachers: The Learning Cycle.**" *Science and Children* Vol. 26(7), 1989: pgs. 30–32.

Beisenherz, Paul C. "**Explore, Invent, and Apply.**" *Science and Children* Vol. 28(4), 1991: pgs. 30–32.

Marek, Edmund A., and Ann M. L. Cavallo. ***The Learning Cycle: Elementary School Science and Beyond.*** Portsmouth, NH: Heinemann, 1997.

National Association for the Education of Young Children (NAEYC). ***Guidelines for Appropriate Curriculum Content and Assessment in Programs Serving Children Ages 3 through 8,*** 1990.

Documenting Learning

The book *Windows on Learning: Documenting Young Children's Work* (Helm, Beneke, and Steinheimer, 1998) begins with this idea: "Documenting children's learning may be one of the most valuable skills a teacher can develop today." The preprimary schools of Reggio Emilia, Italy, have been attracting worldwide attention for more than a decade. In these schools, documentation of children's experience is a standard part of classroom practice. "Documentation practices in Reggio Emilia preprimary schools provide inspiring examples of the importance of displaying children's work with great care and attention to both the content and aesthetic aspects of the display." (Katz, 1996)

Through documentation, teachers help themselves and others see and understand the learning that is taking place. Documentation serves many purposes, providing

- evidence for monitoring each child's growth and development and reliably assessing progress;
- a method of meeting accountability requirements and communicating with parents and administrators;
- evidence to the child of the importance of his or her work to teachers and parents;
- a means of sharing results with children and capturing their interest;
- opportunities to enhance children's memory of their prior work; and
- a mechanism for teachers to evaluate and improve curriculum and teaching methods, thus becoming producers of research.

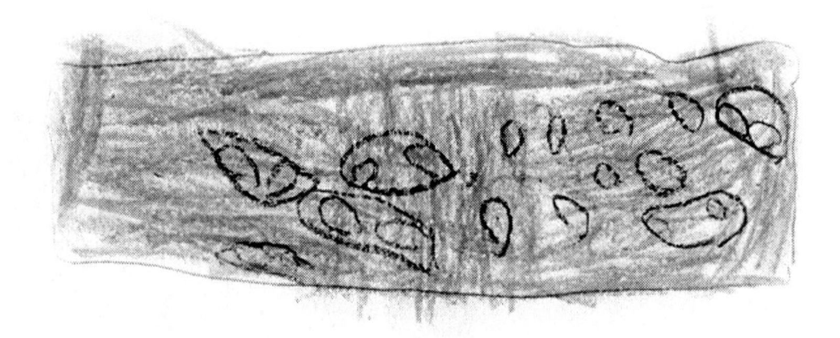

"Documenting Early Science Learning" (Jones and Courtney, 2002) recommends that documentation and assessment of children's work in science follow a five-stage cycle. Teachers begin by identifying science objectives: what children should experience, explore, and understand. Next, teachers collect evidence of children's learning according to three guiding principles:

- **Variety of forms of evidence.** Children vary in how they demonstrate their understanding. Types of evidence collected in early childhood classrooms usually include drawings, drawings with comments dictated to the teacher, photographs, and a record of children's language, particularly in response to open-ended questions.
- **Evidence over a period of time.** A single piece of evidence captures only one moment in time. However, children's understandings of big concepts are not established with a single experience. At a particular moment, a child may be struggling with an idea or question. When added to evidence collected over a period of weeks or months, that single piece of evidence becomes part of a larger picture of development.
- **The understanding of groups of children as well as individuals.** Capturing group conversations at the introduction of a topic can give teachers a sense of what prior experiences, understandings, and misconceptions the group as a whole shares. Science is a social activity, where the sharing of questions, methods, and results is an essential part of the process. Through this sharing, the class as a whole comes to new understandings about a concept. Recording group conversations at the end of a unit can document this outcome.

After collecting evidence of children's learning, the teacher looks closely at the material collected and describes the knowledge represented by the evidence. Doing this step without judgement (such as focusing on what is missing or incorrect) takes practice. Now the children's work can be compared to the standards and goals that the teacher previously identified. Finally, this new information and understanding helps the teacher improve instruction and curriculum.

Some early childhood programs use established methods for documentation and assessment. One popular method is the Work Sampling System. It consists of three complementary components: developmental guidelines and checklists, portfolios of children's work, and summary reports by teachers. Assessments take place three times a year and are meant to place children's work within a broad, developmental perspective. Training to use this system helps teachers develop skills in nonjudgmental recording of behavior. The structure of the system helps teachers organize the collection and evaluation of children's work.

Find Out More

Gandini, Lella. "**Fundamentals of the Reggio Emilia Approach to Early Childhood Education.**" *Young Children* Vol. 49(1), 1993: pgs. 4–8.

Helm, Judy, Sallee Beneke, and Kathy Steinheimer. ***Windows on Learning: Documenting Young Children's Work.*** New York: Teachers College Press, 1998.

Hoisington, Cynthia. "**Using Photographs to Support Children's Science Inquiry.**" *Young Children* Vol. 57(5), 2002: pgs. 26–32.

Jones, Jacqueline, and Rosalea Courtney. "**Documenting Early Science Learning.**" *Young Children* Vol. 57(5), 2002: pgs. 34–40.

Katz, Lilian G. "**Impressions of Reggio Emilia Preschools.**" *Young Children* Vol. 45(6), 1990: pgs. 10–11.

MacDonald-Carlson, Helen. ***Observing and Documenting the Learning Process.*** 1998. The University College of the Cariboo, Kamloops, BC, Canada. Available: http://www.cariboo.bc.ca/SAC/MacDonald_Carlson.htm. May 5, 2003.

Meisels, S.J., et al. ***An Overview: The Work Sampling System.*** Ann Arbor, MI: Rebus Planning Associates, 1994.

Part 8:
All About Sponges

What do scientists know about sponges?

This section includes some interesting background information about the animals we call sponges. You may choose to share some of this information with the children as you find appropriate in your classroom.

Sea Sponges Are Animals

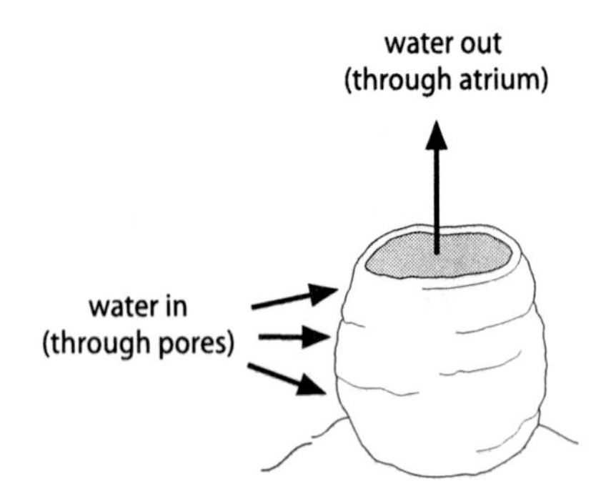

Barrel or vase shape sponge

Are you using animal skeletons to wash with? Before the twentieth century, all sponges that people used were the skeletal remains of primitive sea creatures called, naturally enough, sponges. Today, most household sponges are made from materials such as polyester, rubber, and cellulose (wood fiber) that have been forced with air to create pores.

Sponges have fascinated people for a long time. The ancient Greek philosopher Aristotle found them confusing and couldn't decide whether to classify them as plants or animals. Most sponges don't move and usually spend their lives in colonies attached to rocks on the sea floor or encrusted on the shells of other animals. Many sponges appear as little more than slimy, soft, or prickly layers on rocks. It wasn't until the nineteenth century that scientists realized that sponges eat by filtering microorganisms out of the water—something plants don't do.

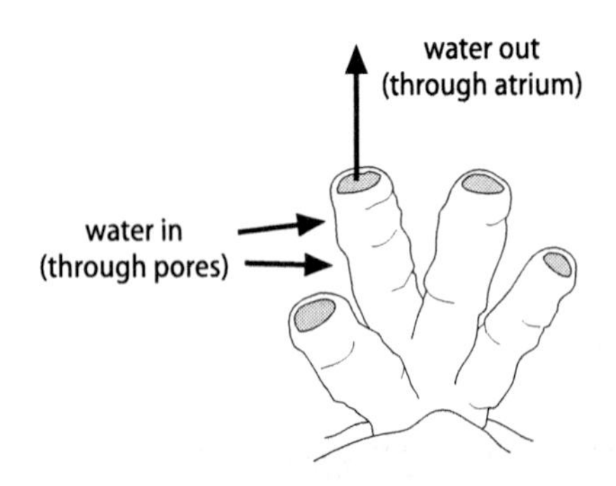

Tube shape sponge

Their Physiology

Sponges belong to the animal group *Porifera,* which means pore bearing. The surface of a sponge is covered with thousands of tiny pores that allow water to flow inside the sponge where individual cells absorb the suspended nutrients. Water entering the pores flows through a system of narrow canals that empty into a group of chambers lined with special cells called choanocytes (kō-ăn' ə-sīts'). These cells capture tiny food particles (bacteria and microalgae) and transfer the nutrients to the other cells. Larger food particles are usually engulfed by cells called pinacocytes (pin-ak' ə-sīts') that line the canals. After the food particles are captured by the choanocytes and pinacocytes, the wastewater is expelled through another series of canals to several large pores called oscula (singular, osculum: ŏs' kyə-ləm). In simple sponges, water leaves the sponge through the osculum. Most sponges are more complex in structure; in these sponges, water flows through oscula into a large chamber called the atrium. Water leaves the sponge through the atrium.

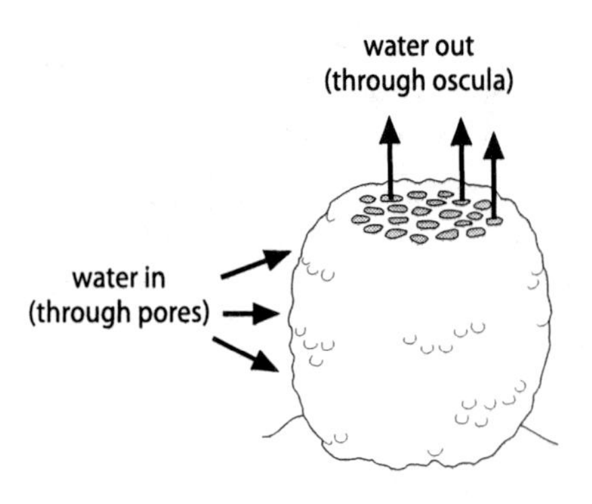

Ball shape sponge

A typical sponge can filter a tremendous quantity of water. For example, one species of the genus *Leucandra,* measuring only 4 inches high by about ½ inch wide, can pump 6 gallons of water a day through its system.

Sponges are the simplest multicellular animals. They have no brain, heart, lungs, or stomach. In fact, a sponge's body lacks any well-defined tissue, consisting only of a loose organization of several types of cells. You can squeeze a live sponge through a fine cloth to separate the cells, and the separated cells, if placed in seawater, will gather together to form a sponge again. If you tried this experiment with another animal, you'd just end up with soup!

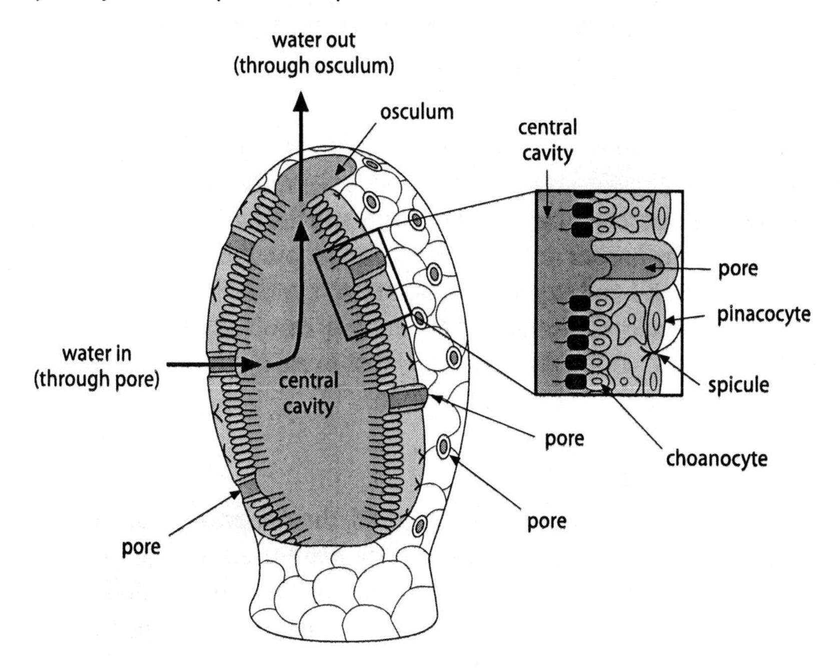

Cross-section of simple sponge

Their Habitat

Sponges may be simple, but they are extremely successful. Scientists have identified over 7,000 different species of sponges living in oceans all over the world, including the icy waters off Antarctica. Most live in shallow waters, but sponges have been found to depths of nearly 20,000 feet below the surface. Some even live in freshwater. At times in Earth's history, sponges have been significant builders of ocean reefs, much like coral today. Fossil sponges date back to the end of the Precambrian era about 600 million years ago and are among the oldest known animal fossils.

Sponges come in an astounding variety of shapes, sizes, and colors. Many are simple tubes or sheets, but they can also be shaped like a tree, sphere, cake, dome, finger, pagoda, fan, trumpet, or vase. Some sponges are large enough that a diver can fit inside them; others are smaller than a grain of rice. Sponges growing on tropical coral reefs can come in colors that include pink, maroon, lemon yellow, orange, red, green, blue, and violet.

The size and shape of a sponge depends not only on its genetic makeup, but also on environmental conditions in the water (for example, the strength and direction of water currents) and can vary greatly even within individual species. Sponges that live in wave-tossed waters often grow in thin crusty layers on the surface of rocks. In deep, quiet waters, glass and tube sponges grow straight upward to avoid fine sediment at the bottom that could clog their pores. In water with slow currents, sponges may spread out in the form of a tree or a fan—a shape that perhaps helps the sponge catch more food.

Their Diet

Though the bulk of their diet comes from filtering particles like bacteria and microscopic algae from seawater, sponges have evolved amazing ways to supplement their food supply. Many species harbor symbiotic bacteria and some harbor microscopic algae that provide the sponge with additional food and oxygen through photosynthesis. Some sponges of the family Cladorhizidae are actually carnivorous and use their spicules (spĭk' yōōls), tiny structures that make up the skeletons of some sponges, to capture small crustaceans.

How We Use Them

Because sponges can soak up so much liquid, they've proved useful to humans throughout history. The early Egyptians used sponges for personal bathing and the Romans used them for paintbrushes and mops. Roman soldiers drank wine from them because they were lighter and easier to carry than metal cups.

Today, natural sponges are still valuable. Painters, window washers, and pottery makers prefer them to manufactured sponges because they last longer and hold more liquid without dripping. The pharmaceutical industry is interested in sponges because of the many potentially beneficial chemicals their bodies produce. Hundreds of chemicals with potential antibiotic, anti-inflammatory, or anticancer activity have already been discovered. Some of these are being developed as drugs. Two drugs, one used for cancer and one used for herpes infections, are based on chemicals produced by a sponge! Sponges have also become part of cultural tradition. In the waters off Japan, a certain species of shrimp spawns within the Venus Flower Basket sponge. The pair of young shrimp develop within the sponge, and as they grow, become too large to leave. The sponge provides them with safety and food for life. In Japan, this type of delicate sponge with its shrimp guests is given as a wedding gift, symbolizing a marriage lasting forever.

Their Appearance

The following pages include photographs of living sponges. You may wish to share these with children to stimulate their interest in natural sponges.

Photograph by Paul Osmond of Deep Sea Images

Giant Barrel Sponge *(Xestospongia muta)*: This picture was taken off the Bimini Islands in the Bahamas. Giant barrel sponges can be found on Caribbean reefs or on the ocean floor next to reefs at depths of 50 to 150 feet. They are often extremely abundant on reefs that slope steadily downward to the ocean floor. Normally giant barrel sponges are 3–4 feet high and 2–3 feet across. A giant barrel sponge this large may be well over a hundred years old, since they typically only grow ½ inch per year. In Florida, one of these sponges was measured to be almost 8 feet high and 6 feet across. This sponge is large enough for a diver to be tempted to climb inside—which a diver should never do. The edges of any sponge are delicate. Breaks in the edges can disrupt the pumping action of the sponge or allow disease organisms to enter the sponge, possibly causing it to die.

Photograph by Paul Osmond of Deep Sea Images

Stove-Pipe Sponge *(Aplysina archeri)*: This image was taken in Roatan, Honduras. These sponges typically inhabit reefs deeper than 80 feet, especially reef walls in the Caribbean. They tend to grow in clusters and can reach a length of 6 feet, although the one in this image is only 2 feet in length.

Photograph by Paul Osmond of Deep Sea Images

Elephant Ear Sponge *(Ianthella basta)*: This specimen was photographed in Milne Bay, Papua New Guinea. Species of elephant ear sponges are common around the world. The pictured species is common to the waters of Papua New Guinea and Australia and is found generally growing on the top of coral reefs no deeper than 100 feet. They can reach sizes of up to 6 feet, although this particular one is about 4 feet in size. This sponge produces chemicals that could be used in medicine.

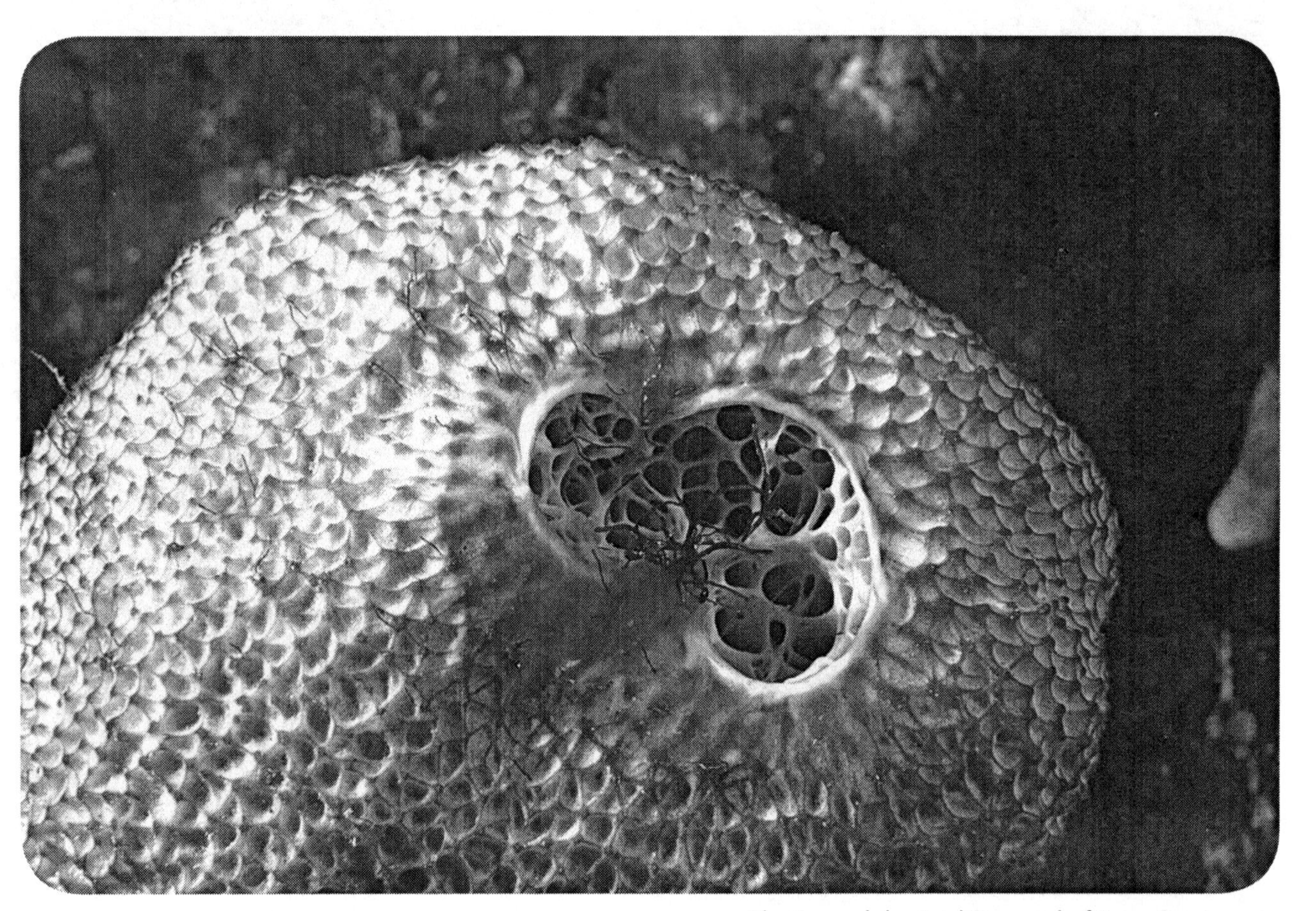

Photograph by Paul Osmond of Deep Sea Images

Ball Sponge *(Ircinia)*: This specimen was photographed in Cozumel, Mexico, and is approximately 1 foot across. Generally, ball sponges inhabit the top of tropical reefs from 40 to 100 feet deep in the Caribbean.

Photograph by Paul Osmond of Deep Sea Images

Brown Tube Sponge *(Agelas conifera)*: This specimen was photographed in a gap between two large reef heads on the reef walls of Cozumel, Mexico, at 80 feet deep. It is approximately 3 feet long and shows the trumpet growth pattern. Brown tube sponges prefer areas protected from heavy currents within reef walls and canyons from about 30 to 130 feet deep. They grow in clusters joined at a base and can grow as large as 4 feet long.

References

American Chemical Society. *Chemistry in the National Science Education Standards: A Reader and Resource Manual for High School Teachers.* Washington, DC, 1997.

Anderson, Robert. *Guide to Florida Corals, Anemones and Sponges.* Winter Springs, FL: Winner Enterprises, 1988.

Ash, Doris, Cappy Greene, and Marilyn Austin. "Inquiry by Teachers." *Connect* Vol. 13(4), 2000: pg. 12.

Barman, Charles R. "Teaching Teachers: The Learning Cycle." *Science and Children* Vol. 26(7), 1989: pgs. 30–32.

Beisenherz, Paul C. "Explore, Invent, and Apply." *Science and Children* Vol. 28(4), 1991: pgs. 30–32.

Bowman, Barbara T., Suzanne M. Donovan, and M. Susan Burns, eds. *Eager to Learn: Educating Our Preschoolers.* Washington, DC: National Academy Press, 2001.

Bredekamp, Sue, and Teresa Rosegrant, eds. *Reaching Potentials: Appropriate Curriculum and Assessment for Young Children.* Vol. 1. Washington, DC: National Association for the Education of Young Children (NAEYC), 1992.

Bresnik, Jane. "Facilitating Inquiry." *Connect* Vol. 13(4), 2000: pgs. 6–8.

Chaille, Christine, and Lory Britain. *The Young Child as Scientist: A Constructivist Approach to Early Childhood Science Education.* Boston: Allyn & Bacon, 2003.

Cheong, Wendy. "The Power of Questioning." *Connect* Vol. 13(4), 2000: pgs. 9–10.

Connect: Inquiry Learning Issue Vol. 8(4), 1995: pgs. 1–20.

Connect: Inquiry Learning Issue Vol. 13(4), 2000: pgs. 1–26.

Edwards, Carolyn, Lella Gandini, and George Forman. *The Hundred Languages of Children: The Reggio Emilia Approach to Early Childhood Education.* Norwood, NJ: Ablex Publishing Corporation, 1993.

Esbensen, Barbara Juster. *Sponges Are Skeletons.* New York: HarperCollins, 1993.

Gandini, Lella. "Fundamentals of the Reggio Emilia Approach to Early Childhood Education." *Young Children* Vol. 49(1), 1993: pgs. 4–8.

Garcia, Eulalia, Andreu Llamas, and Isidro Sanchez. *Sponges: Filters of the Sea.* Milwaukee, WI: Gareth Stevens Publishing, 1997.

Helm, Judy, Sallee Beneke, and Kathy Steinheimer. *Windows on Learning: Documenting Young Children's Work.* New York: Teachers College Press, 1998.

Hoisington, Cynthia. "Using Photographs to Support Children's Science Inquiry." *Young Children* Vol. 57(5), 2002: pgs. 26–32.

Hooper, John, et al. *Sessile Marine Invertebrates.* 2003. Available: http://www.qmuseum.qld.gov.au/organisation/sections/SessileMarineInvertebrates/. March 25, 2003.

Humann, Paul, and Ned Deloach. *Reef Creature Identification: Florida Caribbean Bahamas.* 2nd ed. Jacksonville, FL: New World Publications, 2001.

Jacobson, Morris K. *Wonders of Sponges.* New York: Dodd Mead, 1976.

Jones, Jacqueline, and Rosalea Courtney. "Documenting Early Science Learning." *Young Children* Vol. 57(5), 2002: pgs. 34–40.

Katz, Lilian G. "Impressions of Reggio Emilia Preschools." *Young Children* Vol. 45(6), 1990: pgs. 10–11.

Katz, Lilian G., and Sylvia C. Chard. *The Contribution of Documentation to the Quality of Early Childhood Education.* 1996. ERIC/EECE Clearinghouse on Elementary and Early Childhood Education. Available: http://ericps.crc.uiuc.edu/eece/pubs/digests/1996/lkchar96.html. March 20, 2003.

Kilmer, Sally J., and Helenmarie Hofman. "Transforming Science Curriculum." *Reaching Potentials: Transforming Early Childhood Curriculum and Assessment.* Vol. 2. Washington, DC: National Association for the Education of Young Children, 1995: pgs. 43–63.

Lind, Karen. *Exploring Science in Early Childhood: A Developmental Approach.* Albany, NY: Delmar Publishers, 2000.

Lind, Karen. "Science in Early Childhood: Developing and Acquiring Fundamental Concepts and Skills." Dialogue on Early Childhood Science, Mathematics, and Technology Education. American Association for the Advancement of Science (AAAS), 1999.

Lowery, Lawrence. *The Biological Basis of Thinking and Learning.* Berkeley, CA: Lawrence Hall of Science, 1998.

Lowery, Lawrence. "How New Science Curriculums Reflect Brain Research." *Educational Leadership* Vol. 56(3), 1998: pgs. 26–30.

Lowery, Lawrence. *The Scientific Thinking Process.* Berkeley, CA: Lawrence Hall of Science, 1992.

MacDonald-Carlson, Helen. *Observing and Documenting the Learning Process.* 1998. The University College of the Cariboo, Kamloops, BC, Canada. Available: http://www.cariboo.bc.ca/SAC/MacDonald_Carlson.htm. May 5, 2003.

Marek, Edmund A., and Ann M. L. Cavallo. *The Learning Cycle: Elementary School Science and Beyond.* Portsmouth, NH: Heinemann, 1997.

Meisels, S.J., et al. *An Overview: The Work Sampling System.* Ann Arbor, MI: Rebus Planning Associates, 1994.

Moriarty, Robin. "Entries from a Staff Developer's Journal…Helping Teachers Develop as Facilitators of Three- to Five-Year-Olds' Science Inquiry." *Young Children* Vol. 57(5), 2002: pgs. 20–24.

Mote Marine Laboratory. *About Sponges...* 1993. Available: http://www.marinelab.sarasota.fl.us/SPONGE.HTM. March 25, 2003.

National Association for the Education of Young Children (NAEYC). *Developmentally Appropriate Practice in Early Childhood Programs Serving Children from Birth through Age 8.* 1997. Available: http://www.naeyc.org/resources/position_statements/daptoc.htm. April 25, 2003.

National Association for the Education of Young Children (NAEYC). *Guidelines for Appropriate Curriculum Content and Assessment in Programs Serving Children Ages 3 through 8,* 1990.

National Research Council. *National Science Education Standards: Observe, Interact, Change, Learn.* Washington, DC: National Academy Press, 1996.

Project 2061, ed. *Dialogue on Early Childhood Science, Mathematics, and Technology Education.* Washington, DC: American Association for the Advancement of Science (AAAS), 1999.

University of California Museum of Paleontology. *Introduction to Porifera.* 2003. Available: http://www.ucmp.berkeley.edu/porifera/porifera.html. March 25, 2003.

Villavicencio, Joanna. "Inquiry in Kindergarten." *Connect* Vol. 13(4), 2000: pgs. 3–5.

Woods, Samuel G. *Sorting Out Worms and Other Invertebrates: Everything You Want to Know About Insects, Corals, Mollusks, Sponges and More!* Farmington Hills, MI: Gale Group, 1999.

CPSIA information can be obtained at www.ICGtesting.com
Printed in the USA
LVOW10s1215130814

398930LV00007B/569/P